'By bringing together a range of understandings about transitions, focusing on the timing in life of the primary-secondary transitions and giving real-life examples, this book embraces parents and children, meeting an important gap in the transitions literature in dynamic ways.'

Aline-Wendy Dunlop, *Emeritus Professor, University of Strathclyde, UK*

'This book provides many important recommendations for action and adjustments from a systemic perspective for parents and other important caregivers of the children, presented in an easy-to-understand and theoretically sound manner.'

Daniel Mays, *Professor of Pedagogy, Institute for Special Education, University of Education Freiburg, Germany*

I0024822

SUPPORTING EMOTIONAL WELLBEING DURING PRIMARY-SECONDARY SCHOOL TRANSITIONS

Primary-secondary school transitions mark a pivotal developmental milestone in children's and their supporters' lives. This accessible guide distils international research and practical insights into a reader-friendly resource focused on how parents, carers and teachers can support children's emotional wellbeing during this significant period of change.

Focussing on supporting the supporters, *Supporting Emotional Wellbeing During Primary-Secondary School Transitions* addresses some of the most frequently asked questions about how we can best support our children during this key transitional phase, as well as how we can help them navigate amongst other social, academic, environmental and personal transitions. Following an effective Q&A structure and a 'dip in and out' approach, chapters discuss topics such as puberty and related developmental aspects, support networks, the child's voice, additional support needs and much more. This book includes illustrations and real-life vignettes to help explain some complex concepts and scenarios.

Written by two transitions experts, this essential resource is for parents looking for straightforward guidance on questions related to their child's primary-secondary school transitions. With tips for teachers as well as parents and children, this may also be of interest to educators and school support professionals such as family liaison officers, educational psychologists and teaching assistants.

Charlotte Louise Bagnall is a Senior Lecturer at the University of Manchester within Manchester's Institute of Education.

Divya Jindal-Snape is Professor and Personal Chair of Education, Inclusion and Life Transitions in the School of Humanities, Social Sciences and Law at the University of Dundee.

Bagnall and Jindal-Snape are leading experts in primary-secondary school transitions research and collectively bringing over 30 years of complementary research experience in the field, with a record of knowledge transfer that contributes to well-informed debate, policy and practice nationally and internationally.

BRITISH PSYCHOLOGICAL SOCIETY ASK THE EXPERTS IN PSYCHOLOGY SERIES

Routledge, in partnership with the British Psychological Society (BPS), is pleased to present BPS Ask the Experts, a new popular science series that addresses key issues and answers the burning questions. Drawing on the expertise of established psychologists, every book in the series provides authoritative and straightforward guidance on pressing topics that matter to real people in their everyday lives.

All books in the BPS Ask the Experts series are written for the reader with no prior knowledge or experience. For answers to everything you ever wanted to know about issues important to you, ask the expert!

Rising to the Challenge of Life After Cancer
Expert Advice for Finding Wellness
Jeffrey Charles Dunn and Suzanne Kathleen Chambers

Building a Psychologically Safe Work Environment
Binna Kandola

Understanding Climate Anxiety
Geoffrey Beattie

Living Well with Parkinson's
A Guide to a Fulfilling Life
Angeliki Bogosian

Living with Grief
A Compassionate Companion
Sara Mathews

For more information about this series, please visit: **BPS Ask The Experts in Psychology Series - Book Series - Routledge & CRC Press**

SUPPORTING EMOTIONAL WELLBEING DURING PRIMARY-SECONDARY SCHOOL TRANSITIONS

ADVICE FOR PARENTS, CAREGIVERS AND TEACHERS

CHARLOTTE LOUISE BAGNALL
AND DIVYA JINDAL-SNAPE

Routledge
Taylor & Francis Group

LONDON AND NEW YORK

Designed cover image: Getty Images

First published 2026
by Routledge
4 Park Square, Milton Park, Abingdon, Oxon OX14 4RN

and by Routledge
605 Third Avenue, New York, NY 10158

Routledge is an imprint of the Taylor & Francis Group, an informa business

For Product Safety Concerns and Information please contact our
EU representative GPSR@taylorandfrancis.com. Taylor & Francis
Verlag GmbH, Kaufingerstraße 24, 80331 München, Germany.

Trademark notice: Product or corporate names may be trademarks
or registered trademarks, and are used only for identification and
explanation without intent to infringe.

British Library Cataloguing-in-Publication Data
A catalogue record for this book is available from the British Library

ISBN: 9781032716121 (hbk)
ISBN: 9781032715773 (pbk)
ISBN: 9781032716145 (ebk)

DOI: 10.4324/9781032716145

Typeset in Joanna
by codeMantra

To our parents and grandparents for supporting us during our numerous transitions

CONTENTS

FIGURES

BOXES

ACKNOWLEDGEMENTS

We wish to extend our sincere gratitude to our research participants who have generously given their time and shared their excellent insights about primary-secondary school transitions and emotional wellbeing.

We would like to thank Molly Selby (Routledge) and Rachel… (British Psychological Society) for their feedback and ongoing support.

Finally, we would like to express our love and thanks to our families for their unwavering support and patience.

WHO ARE WE AND WHY ARE WE GIVING YOU THIS ADVICE

First and foremost, Divya is a mother with lived experience of her two children's primary-secondary school transitions and her related transitions experiences in supporting them. The chapters tap into those experiences in terms of what parents might want to know, along with three decades of complementary research experience within the field.

Charlotte is a Senior Lecturer at the University of Manchester within Manchester's Institute of Education. She also holds international visiting research fellowships at the University of Melbourne, Flinders' University and the Black Dog Institution in Australia. She also sits on the British Psychological Society Educational Psychology Section Committee and The Centre for Transformative Change: Educational and Life Transitions (TCELT) Board.

Divya is a Professor of Education, Inclusion and Life Transitions at the University of Dundee, Scotland. She setup TCELT, an International Network of Transitions Researchers and International Journal of Educational and Life Transitions She is also Adjunct Professor at Universitas Sriwijaya, Indonesia, and Visiting Professor at the University of Bristol and Cardiff Metropolitan University. She was also visiting senior researcher at Waseda University, Japan, in 2022. Before this, Divya was a schoolteacher in India and undertook her PhD in Japan. Divya is the only transitions researcher in the world who studies different types of transitions. Her transitions research spans from cradle to grave as well as covering different educational stages. This expertise in different types of transitions led to her development of two transitions theories, Educational and Life Transitions (ELT) Theory and Multiple and Multi-dimensional Transitions (MMT) Theory. She is currently working on a research handbook for Palgrave, which focuses on MMT Theory with authors around the world showing how they have used the theory in their research and practice. We have also used the theory in this book to highlight parents' and professionals' own transitions, and that you need transitions support too.

Charlotte is an applied psychologist within education and has a particular interest in intervention science and co-creation within transitions research. She is particularly passionate about primary-secondary school transitions and how we can improve children's emotional wellbeing during this time, taking an early preventative approach, and has worked with several Local Authorities and schools nationally and also internationally to design, implement and evaluate support provision. From a policy perspective, her approach to supporting children's emotional wellbeing over primary-secondary school transitions has been referenced in policy guidelines for the BBC (2024), NICE (07/22), Health Policy Scotland Guidelines (01/20) and the Department for Education in both England and Australia; with her #_TaST_ intervention being referenced as a "promising universal intervention to improve children's emotional wellbeing over primary-secondary school transitions". Charlotte and Divya are now currently designing a scale (#_P-S WELLS_) for practitioners and researchers to examine children's emotional wellbeing during this time, which is currently being validated across the UK and Australia and is discussed in this book.

In the context of educational stages, and more specifically primary-secondary school transitions, both Charlotte and Divya have undertaken several seminal international reviews of literature and studies where we collected data first-hand or analysed already existing large datasets. Knowing from their own experience that parents and professionals do not have the time to read a book or article and then have to work out how to use the learning from it, they have designed several educational resources based on our research to support transitions, which you can find here. They have to admit that is their favourite part of what they do! You can see some examples of that in this book, and They have really relished this opportunity to write for parents too. In 2016, Divya also wrote a book for professionals, namely A-Z of Transitions, which has received positive feedback from professionals from different disciplines and sectors across the world.

From a personal perspective, this is Charlotte's first book, whereas for Divya (Charlotte's mentor, academic mum, lifelong friend and inspiration), it is one of her last before retirement. Writing this book has been a fantastic opportunity to reflect on our research, both emerging for Charlotte and for Divya her legacy, and they have thoroughly enjoyed writing together in an area and style that they are passionate about. What can be better for a researcher than to be able to write a book that translates their research into conversations with parents and professionals! As if they are standing at the school gates and discussing different aspects of primary-secondary school transitions that they have learnt through their research over the years, including what works, what doesn't work, what they would have loved to know sooner. They have tried to recreate that atmosphere in this book through a series of questions that you might have and then tried to respond to them. Hope you enjoy reading this book and find it useful in supporting your child's and your own transitions.

1

WHAT ARE PRIMARY-SECONDARY SCHOOL TRANSITIONS AND WHAT DO I NEED TO KNOW?

INTRODUCTION

We will start this chapter with a discussion of what transitions mean. This will include a discussion of multiple transitions, as your child will typically experience multiple transitions at the same time when they start secondary school, such as academic and social transitions. The chapter also focuses on what successful primary-secondary school transitions look like and provides some top tips that you can use to support the child and your own transitions, as well as the child supporting their own transitions.

Throughout the book, we will refer to some children, parents, carers and teachers whose narratives have been crafted as vignettes based on the conversations we have had with numerous people over the years. These vignettes will aid in providing real-life examples, and you will be able to better hear their voices. Please note that pseudonyms have been used throughout.

We also want to acknowledge that when using the term 'parents', we are making reference to parents, guardians and carers.

DOI: 10.4324/9781032716145-1

VIGNETTE 1.1. WHEN ALEX STARTS SECONDARY SCHOOL: MULTIPLE CHANGES

Alex will be starting secondary school in two months' time. They have started to think about everything that will change for them. They said:

> I will be moving to Newton High soon. This will be a big change for me as I have been at Hawthorne Primary for seven years and have only been to Newton High twice.
>
> Some of my friends are going to other schools. I also had good friends in other classes at Hawthorne as we played hockey together. I will miss them! Saying that, I am also looking forward to making new friends. I want to be a new me and not stay in the same friendship groups as before.
>
> What I am most excited about is having more subjects and different teachers, better gym and lab…you know, there is a massive swimming pool! But what if I get lost?

Alex said that all these changes were exciting but worrying too, especially as they will be happening at the same time. Also, they found that a lot of changes were taking place elsewhere too. For instance, the sports club they were going to for the last four years is only open up to the age of 12, and they will have to find a different club. This again means that they will not only lose another familiar environment but also some friends.

However, Alex said they were confident they could manage these changes:

> Me and my grandpa were talking about it the other day. This is the same as when I started primary school, isn't

it? Or when my baby brother was born? Or when due to COVID we had to study at home and could not meet our friends for some time? And couldn't meet grandpa of course as he was shielding.

WHAT ARE PRIMARY-SECONDARY SCHOOL TRANSITIONS?

The reason Alex is feeling confident about managing these multiple, concurrent changes and related transitions is that they realise that they have successfully managed them before. It is true that when we experience a change or multiple changes, if they aren't expected, we might end up feeling like a rabbit caught in the headlights! However, changes related to educational stages are known to children and families in most countries, and we prepare for them continuously. Parents and grandparents have experienced them, and although some aspects of schools and education system might change, most stay the same. Children like Alex would have seen older children from their primary school start secondary school too.

Most importantly, whether we experience expected or unexpected changes, we naturally start trying to adapt to them. This **adaptation process**, which doesn't happen in one day, certainly not on what schools call 'Transition Days', but over time, is known as **transitions**. Some countries and researchers have helpfully distinguished between the move or transfer to secondary school and transitions to and through secondary school. Therefore, as we move forward in our discussions about primary-secondary school transitions, we are referring to **transitions as an ongoing, adaptation process** that is triggered by the multiple changes the child or you would experience (Jindal-Snape, 2016). The term **move or transfer** will be used to refer to the **actual physical process** of relocating to another school (Galton et al., 2003).

To summarise, primary-secondary school transitions can be defined as an ongoing process of adaptation due to changes in context/s, namely, primary and secondary school, home, social clubs, community, etc. Similarly, these adaptations will happen in multiple domains, such as psychological domain with links with emotional wellbeing (see Chapters 2 and 3 for more detail), or academic where the child might find that the difficulty level or expectation of academic work has changed (Jindal-Snape, 2016, 2018, 2023).

It is important for us as parents and professionals to remember that as transitions are an ongoing process, children have ongoing/emerging transitions support needs. Therefore, transitions support should also be provided in an ongoing manner at school and at home. However, as we know from our own experience and research, schools typically provide support when children are towards the end of the final year of primary school and the first few months of the first year in secondary school (Jindal-Snape & Cantali, 2019). This implies that the schools are treating transitions as an event of 'moving/starting school', i.e., transfer, rather than an ongoing process (Jindal-Snape, 2016).

VIGNETTE 1.2. WHEN SUCCESSFUL TRANSITIONS LOOK DIFFERENT

Jenny and Lisa both started secondary school at the same time and in the same local authority but in different schools. When we met them after they had started secondary school, they were both finding the transitions difficult due to the bullying they were experiencing, and this was having an impact on their emotional wellbeing. They were being supported by their families, guidance staff, as well as, in this case, their community link workers.

We met them three months later. Jenny had left their original secondary school and moved to a different secondary school. They said:

> I have only been at the new school for six weeks but have already made two friends. The stress every night and every

morning of having to go to my old school and how I might be bullied was making me hate school. I was feeling sick all the time. Now, although I am still a bit nervous at the new school, I am less scared. Yes, you could say that I am a bit happier even.

Lisa had stayed in the same school. They told us:

I am still bullied from time to time and that makes me really upset… almost every day. But I am a fighter, you know. I told my family that I will not quit the school because of some nasty children! My guidance teacher has said I can sit in their classroom at lunchtime as that is when I am most bullied. I have got to know one child quite well as they go there too. I have also got to know a couple of teachers quite well. They are really nice.

Now the question is, who do you think was having successful transitions? Jenny who left the secondary school to find a better fit or Lisa who had persisted in adapting to that particular school?
    Let's discuss this a bit further.

WHAT ARE SUCCESSFUL PRIMARY-SECONDARY SCHOOL TRANSITIONS?

The problem with the term **successful transitions** is that we all talk about it, but very rarely do we check who means what when they use the term. This is the same in transitions literature. In the past, research has focussed on unsuccessful transitions as seen by dips in attainment, motivation and engagement, and increase in negative attitudes towards subjects and school. By default, then, it was assumed that a child was having successful transitions when there were no dips in attainment or children were positive about subjects/school and were motivated and engaged (Evangelou et al., 2008).

However, think about what is most important to a parent or child when the child moves to secondary school? What are you wanting to know when you meet your child's secondary school teacher at a parents' evening at school? Do you want to know how good your child's academic performance is? Or do you want to know whether the child is happy in the new school? Have they made friends? Have they developed good relationships with teachers?

The parents and children we spoke with were more focussed on the child feeling connected, having a sense of belonging at the school, and developing meaningful, positive and respectful relationships with their peers and multiple teachers in the secondary school (Ashton, 2008; Jindal-Snape, 2016, 2023). This seems to be the case, especially in the early days of starting the new school. Once the child has adapted to the various changes resulting from the transfer and feel happy and settled in, both parents' and child's focus might change, for example, to academic aspects. Of course, it could then change back to the social and relationships aspects when they move to the next year group.

Unfortunately, in practice, there can be a mismatch between the views of families and teachers about what successful transitions are. Interestingly, in Jenny's case (see Vignette 1.2), the initial secondary school saw them as having unsuccessful transitions, despite them 'choosing' the second school and being happier there. However, Lisa's school saw them as having some success with their transitions as they had not left that school, despite still being bullied, although the intensity had reduced.

What are your thoughts about their transitions? Who was having successful transitions? The reality is that it is not up to us to decide what constitutes successful transitions for whom. It is for the individual to decide, as we are all unique and will have our own views on this. In this instance, from our discussions with Jenny and Lisa, we know that they were both feeling they had had some success with their transitions.

Therefore, it is important that there is clear communication between child, family and teachers about what successful transitions mean to that *particular child*, that *particular family* or that *particular teacher*. It is important that children have a clear voice in this and for them to have opportunities to discuss this over time as their own perceptions might change.

WHY ARE PRIMARY-SECONDARY SCHOOL TRANSITIONS GIVEN SO MUCH ATTENTION?

Throughout our life, we go through many transitions. They are all important and have an impact on our life course and emotional wellbeing. So why is it that there is so much discussion about primary-secondary school transitions? Is our focus on these transitions disproportionate compared to other transitions? These are really important questions to ask.

If you look at transitions research, you will find that primary-secondary school transitions are the most researched transitions. If you look at policy and practice, again a lot of work has gone into getting primary-secondary school transitions right. However, if we look at the research 'evidence', one would feel that nothing has worked or only to a limited extent (see Chapter 4).

Where have we gone wrong? We think there are several reasons for this, including (i) lack of an agreed view of what primary-secondary school transitions are, (ii) the research on which practice and policy are based has several limitations, (iii) a mistaken belief that we have dealt with the pastoral aspect quite well and we now need to focus on fixing the curricular and attainment side of things, (iv) they happen when children are going through multiple developmental transitions and (v) there is a negative discourse surrounding them.

If you look at Figure 1.1, you can see that when we all go with our own understanding of something without a discussion of others' understanding of it, the object we are focussing on can look very different to the reality. This, for instance, means that if a school and professionals see transitions as the move from primary to secondary school, transitions planning and practices might start just before and

Figure 1.1 Perceptions in silo. Art: Graham Ogilvie

after the move to secondary school. If the school and professionals see transitions as an ongoing process, they are more likely to start planning and preparing children from an earlier stage and carry on providing support beyond the first few months, and even across, secondary school. We will come back to this in Chapter 5.

Most research literature does not paint a positive picture of primary-secondary school transitions (Jindal-Snape et al., 2020). Researchers have highlighted the negative impact of primary-secondary school transitions on:

i. children's academic outcomes, due to dip in attainment, including negative attitudes towards certain subjects and high dropout rates
ii. children's wellbeing, due to increase in stress and anxiety and an increase in problem behaviours
iii. children dropping out of secondary school

Based on their longitudinal study in which they followed the same children throughout secondary school, West et al. (2010) reported that the negative impact of children's primary-secondary school transitions can be long term, such as on their mental health. However, they have also argued that any evidence of the negative impacts can be contested as **co-existing** but not necessarily providing a cause-and-effect relationship. This means that if we observe a dip in attainment when children start secondary school, we can't be sure that it is due to primary-secondary school transitions.

These research findings will possibly be of concern to you. However, it is important that you are aware that there are several limitations to the research literature, such as small sample size, data collection immediately before and after children move to secondary school, etc. Also, we don't know what motivated those researchers to undertake those studies. Were they invited by schools to undertake the study and follow particular children, as problems with transitions were observed? Did the researchers initiate the research but asked the school, or the schools decided, to select children who were experiencing problems? The former was the case with one of our studies where the schools had nominated particular children to be part of the study as they wanted to improve outcome for those who were experiencing difficulties. Further, as discussed later, studies don't indicate the proportion of children who had positive or negative transitions experiences.

This is especially of concern as there are several positive aspects to the transitions to secondary school which get lost in this louder negative discourse, such as, children's progression across key educational stages, and benefits of more choices and opportunities that a larger secondary school can offer, including more teachers and peers to create positive relationships with, different subjects that would enable a child to study subjects of their interest, a wider variety of sports to choose from and better resources and facilities for educational and co-curricular activities.

The studies that have indicated the proportion of children who had negative transitions found that almost 1 child in 3 is likely to have had a negative transition, at least at some time during these transitions. This highlights the importance of ensuring that children have successful primary-secondary school transitions, especially as they can have an impact at some point on every child's academic, psychological and life transitions. Therefore, it is important that parents and teachers focus on every child as an individual who might have a transition experience that is very different from others and be mindful of where in their primary-secondary school transitions journey they are. Also, as discussed later in Chapter 4, it is important that they hear a balanced discourse about transitions both from parents and teachers.

There is some complacency and misguided belief amongst schools, thinking that they have done enough work to resolve pastoral matters so the focus should be on resolving the curricular continuity and improving attainment. There is, perhaps, a perception that they can be resolved separately and just because some pastoral support worked for some children, they will also work for other children, despite the uniqueness of everyone's background and experiences. However, there are some really good practices where these aspects have been considered and brought together (see Vignette 2.1).

As can be seen from Vignette 5.2, in Chapter 5, schools can effectively create projects to support transitions that can ensure the following:

 i. curricular continuity from primary to secondary school,
 ii. continuity of pedagogical approaches of primary and secondary school teachers,
iii. interdisciplinary working,
 iv. children being able to choose to work according to their strengths, ensuring building of confidence and self-esteem (children having to help the teacher in setting up consoles also added to this),
  v. quick relationship building which endured across secondary school due to being put in a team to work collectively to achieve something and
 vi. a positive platform for the first meeting with their guidance and subject teachers.

Therefore, it is not a matter of choosing one aspect of transitions over others but rather focussing on them collectively in a way that one builds upon the other.

Finally, another reason for primary-secondary school transitions getting so much attention is that they happen at a very large scale around the world (which in some ways sounds strange because the same scale must have applied to starting primary school!). Every year, millions of children around the world start secondary school or equivalent (Jindal-Snape et al., 2023b). It is a massive enterprise in its own right! This enterprise also keeps businesses afloat, such as those providing school uniforms, film franchises, publishers, etc. It is a market that is flooded with negative discourse and potential quick 'fixes' by some consultants and researchers.

However, we don't want you to think that we don't believe primary-secondary school transitions aren't important. They are hugely important, not the least because they can have long-term consequences on other educational and life transitions, with an impact on improving or deteriorating children's emotional wellbeing (see Chapters 2 and 3). If we think in a child-centred manner, perhaps this is the most important reason for focussing on primary-secondary school transitions, not the least because it has been found that those who had negative primary-secondary school transitions had mental health issues later in life (West et al., 2010). The links between emotional wellbeing and academic attainment are not conclusive but they co-exist too (Jindal-Snape et al., 2020).

WHAT DOES A PARENT NEED TO KNOW ABOUT THEIR CHILD'S TRANSITIONS?

MULTIPLE TRANSITIONS

As mentioned earlier, a child will go through multiple transitions on the same day, potentially every day. These could include transitions due to moving from one classroom to another, change in teacher/s for each period, and change in peers who will be in each of those classes. These have been referred to as horizontal transitions, i.e., transitions they experience every day (Pietarinen et al., 2010). The term vertical transitions has also been used to describe those related to moving from primary to secondary school. It is an interesting way of understanding their transitions. Most importantly, they will be navigating multiple such horizontal transitions every day between all the spaces they occupy, e.g., at home or a sports club in the community.

SCENARIO 1.3 MANAGING UNEXPECTED CHANGES

A group of children are in the playground. Sammy comes outside from the classroom and a soft rubber ball comes flying towards them. It takes them by surprise and they are unable to catch it or get out of the way. They then notice that the group is playing a game of throwing balls for others to catch. No rules are discussed but Sammy is happy that they know what to do. They are prepared for the ball this time and catch it easily. They are smiling and enjoying the game. Suddenly, without discussion, the rules seem to change with multiple balls being thrown at different children, including Sammy. Sammy catches as many as they can but are looking overwhelmed with so many balls coming at them from all directions. Due to being overwhelmed, they end up dropping the two balls they had managed to catch.

As previously mentioned in Alex's case, they were aware of some changes that they will experience and felt ready to successfully manage them. They have most likely rehearsed and prepared for them throughout their life and have had discussions with their families, friends and teachers. However, when these changes are unexpected, like for Sammy, they can take more time to adapt to (See Scenario 1.3). Most importantly, whether these changes are expected or unexpected, when they come from all directions at the same time, they can unsurprisingly be overwhelming for the child. Therefore, it is important for parents and teachers to be mindful of the multiple

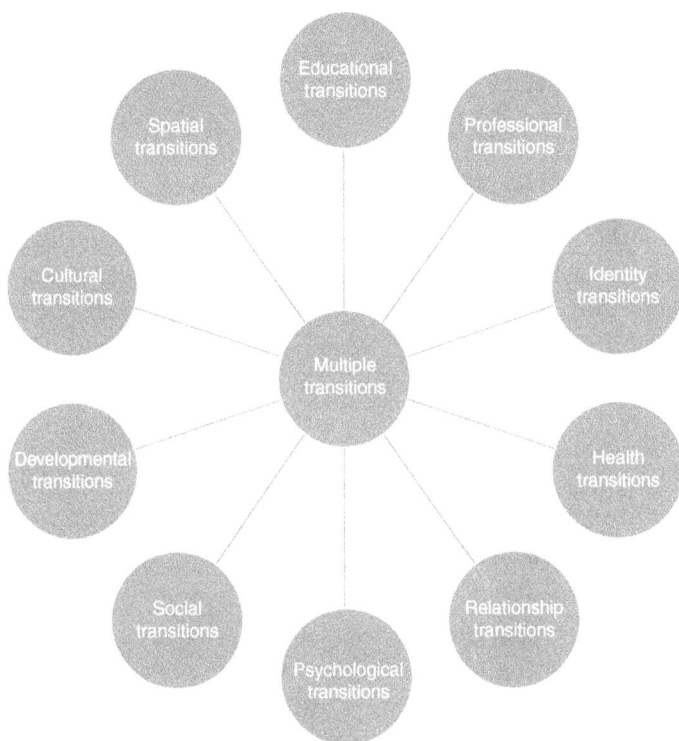

Figure 1.2 Examples of multiple transitions that children and adults might experience.

transitions these multiple changes will trigger for the child (see Figure 1.2 for some examples of multiple transitions children and adults might experience).

Where possible, multiple changes should be minimised or at least staggered a bit. For example, familiarisation with the school building and spaces can be done much earlier through primary school children using the gym or labs of the secondary school they might attend. Of course, not all educational systems have the catchment area or feeder school system, so children might not always know which secondary school they will attend. Even when this was the case, we found having the experience of going to *any* secondary school whilst in primary helped children feel confident about being able to manage the larger environment of their new secondary school (Jindal-Snape & Cantali, 2019).

EXCITED AND WORRIED AT THE SAME TIME

Like Alex, you will find that your child/ren can be excited about moving to the secondary school as well as worried at the same time. For instance, a child might look forward to starting secondary school due to better access to sports facilities but be worried about being the smallest in the gym or not as good at sports as the other, potentially more senior children, at the same time (see Figure 1.3).

Some other aspects can be:

* Looking forward to making new friends but worrying about whether they will be able to make new friends and about losing their primary school friends.

Looking forward to having several subject specialist teachers instead of just one teacher teaching them all the subjects in primary school; worrying about losing the trusted and well-developed relationship with a primary school teacher to having to engage with multiple secondary school teachers for very short periods of time every week.

Figure 1.3 Change in a child's perception of being the oldest to being the youngest after starting secondary school.

Source: Jindal-Snape et al., 2023; Art: Clio Ding.

Looking forward to a larger secondary school with better facilities for sports, arts, music and lunches; worrying about getting lost in the large school and being punished by teachers for being late to classes.

However, we also found that, reassuringly, after starting secondary school, the things they were excited about were still seen by them as aspects that were good about secondary school. Further, they stayed positive about them even at the end of two years of secondary school (Jindal-Snape & Cantali, 2019). Conversely, aspects they were worried about were not as worrying when they started secondary school; although some concerns did emerge as they were starting the second year of secondary school, such as moving away from some classmates and having to make new friends.

Therefore, it is important that we make children aware that aspects they are worrying about when in primary school might not be worrying in reality (also see Vignette 1.5). Further, it is important to emphasise that most children adapt very well to the secondary school over time.

WHAT DOES A PARENT NEED TO KNOW ABOUT THE IMPACT OF AGE AND TIMING OF SCHOOL TRANSITIONS? WHY?

Across the globe, staged, age-graded educational transitions generally occur between the ages of 10 and 15 years, and during this time, children can make two-tier or three-tier school transfers. School transfers tiers are predetermined by the Local Authority, and in the UK, most regions align with the two-tier educational system, where children navigate the move from primary school to secondary school at age 11. However, across the UK, there are 29 middle schools (DfE, 2024; Scottish Government, 2025), which align with three-tier educational transfers. During these systems, children begin education in a first school, or lower school, which educates children up to the age 9 (Year 4 in England and Wales, and P4 in Scotland). Children then make their first school transfer to a middle school, which caters for children up to the age of 15 (Year 9 in England and S3 in Scotland). Following this, children make their second school transfer to an upper school or high school.

To date, there is no consensus internationally or even within individual countries on the most appropriate age and timing for children to make these school transfer, despite commissioned research starting in the 1920s in England. For example, research (including Charlotte's) has suggested that generally children who are older when navigating school transfer show more positive social, academic and emotional adjustment. The reason for this is that the older children are when they make school transfer, the more likely they have been exposed to previous life transitions, such as moving to a new house, parent divorce, birth of a new sibling, bereavement, and as a result can adapt to similar challenges inherent in school transitions, such as school environment adaptations (e.g., moving between lessons for different subjects), more easily.

Moreover, when transfer timing is delayed, such as school transfer from middle school to high school in the USA at age 14, children have had longer to gain developmental skills, such as emotional intelligence, necessary to successfully navigate challenges inherent in school transitions more easily, whether that is disagreements with peers, environmental discontinuities such as getting lost or academic changes indicative of the new ways of learning. For example, middle schools (that teach children from age 9 to age 14 in the UK, and 11–14 in the USA) have advantages over secondary schools, by providing children with consistency, in terms of being taught by the same trusted teacher and in a stable school environment, with the same pastoral support, which is often more sensitive and focused on this developmental age. This can be helpful for children during early puberty, as expressed by a parent in my own case study research in the USA (Bagnall et al., 2021, p. 360): "I mean during the time when they're in the most turmoil, they would have more consistency in an Elementary level you know with one teacher or people who know them" (Parent of child in K-8 Elementary School). This parent went on to say that they felt their child's transitions to high school will be easier because of how emotionally settled they were in their K-8 elementary school and ready to navigate these transitions.

Similar research undertaken in the UK by Symonds and Hargreaves (2016), who conducted interviews over a one-year period with two same-aged groups of children, who had either transferred into their first year of secondary school (transitions sample), or remained in their third year of middle school (non-transitions sample). It was found that children who navigated school transfer experienced more negative emotional and motivational engagement, which shaped children's feelings of enjoyment, social conflict, companionship, relatedness and autonomy. Insights from two-tier and three-tier school transfer in Australia shed further light on these findings, in that girls were significantly more anxious in Year 7 at high school compared to their K-10 counterparts (Nguyen et al., 2017). However, after eight months of Year 7, children who navigated a three-tier educational system were shown to fare better academically and socially in terms of student-student relations. This demonstrates the need to examine outcomes over time, given the instability of this period, which is in line with the Multiple and Multi-dimensional (MMT) Theory, discussed in detail later.

As mentioned previously, children's voices are relatively unexplored within the field, despite consistent recommendations to do so endorsing the importance of valuing their first-hand insight and involving them in decision-making. When thinking about the age and timing of educational transitions, research which has listened to children's voices (including Charlotte's) has shown that children generally prefer three-tier school transfer, as they find transitioning to their third school easier, reflecting the insight and skills gained from their first transitions. For example, reflecting on the two-tier

K-8 educational system vs. three-tier middle or junior high school educational system in the USA, one Grade 9 child said:

> there's just a bigger leap, there's a bigger gap between K-8 to High school, you're gonna keep them little longer and then all of a sudden they're thrown in with seniors and they didn't get to transition and kind of come into their own of being independent, making their own decisions, they're still kind of under the guise of you're little.
>
> (Bagnall et al., 2021, p. 361)

In other words, children felt three-tier systems can provide children with exposure, self-assurance and confidence into what high school transitions will be like, and opportunity to test-out and practice problem-solving and coping-skills.

In sum, these two ideas (transitions timing and age) are in conflict, as while transition appears to be better the older children are, but then the transition, when it happens, is a bigger 'leap'. This might be more noticeable in the USA because children have navigated different systems, with those within the K-8 system appearing to other children and adults as not quite as prepared for the move as children within the junior high or middle school system. However, this makes it unclear in understanding which school system is best for children and the optimal age for school transitions.

However, what we can take from this research as a parent is the importance of developing children's understanding of educational transitions and exposure to challenge and discontinuity, which they might experience over the school transfer, such as asking for help and making decisions. During these experiences, it is important to scaffold, practice and testing-out children's problem-solving skills, within a safe child-led environment. Throughout, focus should be placed on nurturing continuity and progression, and presenting transitions as a time of developmental growth as opposed to loss (see Chapter 5 for some useful activities).

WHAT DOES A PARENT NEED TO KNOW ABOUT HOW PUBERTY AND RELATED DEVELOPMENT ASPECTS PARTICULARLY INTERSECT AT THE TIME OF SCHOOL TRANSITIONS?

Look at Vignette 1.4 for Sammy and Jade's experience. Jade had made arrangements at work to be able to drive Sammy to his secondary school every day, at least for the first few months. However, Sammy though grateful at the start, wanted to make their own way to school. Why do you think that might be? When children are moving to secondary school, in most countries, it is during puberty. As you will know from your own experience, puberty is a period when children experience rapid physical, social, emotional and psychological changes (Symonds et al., 2024). You will also have observed that the start of puberty and its development can be different for boys and girls. This is the period when children have a need to assert autonomy, especially from their parents; want to develop friendships but also sexual relationships; want to develop new identit/ies (see Alex's comment in Vignette 1.1); along with changes in feelings of self-esteem. Overall, this means that children are not only experiencing educational transitions but also multiple unrelated transitions due to their developmental stage.

Eccles and colleagues (e.g., Eccles et al., 1993; Gutman & Eccles, 2007) have used the lens of Stage-Environment Fit Theory to explain the necessity of the environment (and those situated in them, i.e., family, teachers) to align with the child's pubertal and adolescence stage. For instance, if there is a mismatch between the child's wish for autonomy with that of their parents and/or teachers, who might be perceived to be controlling, it can lead to anxiety and stress for the child and also lead to strained relationships with them.

Do you remember the feeling of being considered a child in one context and an adult in another during puberty? I Divya remember being 14 years old and going to a birthday party where there were children and adults. A game of musical chairs was organised.

I was asked to not join the children's round of musical chairs as was *a couple of years older* than the child whose birthday it was and their friends, and it wouldn't be fair for them to compete with me. When I went to join the adults' round, adults protested that it wasn't fair for me to compete with them as I would win being so much younger than them. It meant that I was not allowed to join either group and still remember feeling very upset and excluded. This meant that for others my identity was dependent on who else was in that environment. I was the same person; however, others saw me according to their own measure of whether I was a child or an adult, and not how I saw myself. The fact that I can still visualise clearly what happened that day four decades plus later highlights how sensitive we can be when going through puberty, and being neither this nor that in other people's eyes.

Imagine a scenario where Jade had insisted on driving Sammy to school, as apart from anything else Sammy taking the bus meant everyone having to wake up earlier every morning and her having to go back to her workplace to ask for a change in her shifts again. How do you think it would have played out? Or in the case of Jenny, what if her family had insisted they stayed in the same secondary school, or Lisa's parents insisted they left that particular secondary school and moved elsewhere (Vignette 1.2)? Even though their routes were different both Jenny and Lisa had later felt their transitions were going better, and this, undoubtedly in part at least, was linked to having choice, autonomy, a say in what they wanted to happen.

Therefore, it is important that at home and school, we can create an environment which promotes (and signals to the child) autonomy, giving them freedom on matters that are important to them, and listen to their voice. Most importantly, this requires a shift in our own sense of identity and the dynamics in your relationship with the child, with you learning to let go of control. This inevitably means transitions for the adults in the life of the child, like we saw in Jade's case.

WHAT IS THE SIGNIFICANCE OF NAVIGATING MULTIPLE TRANSITIONS ACROSS DOMAINS (E.G., EDUCATIONAL, PSYCHOLOGICAL) AND CONTEXTS (E.G., HOME, SCHOOL)?

When a child moves from one class to another within the same school (such as one year of primary school to the next year), they still need to adapt to potentially a different class teacher or room but most of the other aspects are the same, such as their peers, school building and staff members. Although there will be changes, the stability of other aspects of their school life will most likely support them in dealing with them successfully. However, when moving to secondary school, the only constant might be their family, friends in the neighbourhood and peers at any out-of-school clubs/activities they are part of. No wonder children in our studies have highlighted family and friends to be their strongest support networks (Jindal-Snape & Cantali, 2019).

As mentioned earlier, children will be experiencing multiple transitions in multiple domains. For example, they will experience developmental transitions at the same time as they will experience transitions in the psychological domain (both due to their developmental stage and related to excitement, stress and anxiety related to starting secondary school). They will, at the same time, experience educational transitions due to moving a year above as well as potential differences in pedagogical approaches and assessment and high volume of homework given by teachers in some secondary schools. Further, when moving to secondary school, they will also find that relationships at school are in a state of flux. They will experience transitions in the social domain, both related to losing old and making new relationships with peers and teachers. As we saw in Alex's case, all of these will both excite and worry them (see Vignette 1.1). However, the most important aspect is that they will be managing multiple transitions at the same time. Where possible, it is important that certain aspects of their life are stable, such as in the contexts outside school.

What we have described just now is primarily related to the school context. That is, of course, not the only context they will find themselves in throughout one day. They will be at home, go to a drama club perhaps, and/or Scouts/Guides, to name a few. All of these contexts have their own (usually hidden) rules and culture. It might be acceptable for the child to run around a room in one context but not another. They might be encouraged to speak very loudly in one space but told to ask permission before speaking in another. The child has to navigate these multiple contexts in the same day, and several times. A child will inhabit multiple spaces with complexities attached to each one (Jindal-Snape, 2016). The child then has to learn to negotiate differences in their rules and cultures. This might require them to adopt one identity at home and another at school.

Also, it is important to remember that any impact of these transitions is so subtle and ongoing that even the individual might not notice them, let alone others. Using the metaphor of a waterfall – where the waterfall might seem the same but the water flowing through it is never the same – we can visualise the impact of transitions over time. Therefore, although we might 'see' the individual as being 'Angie', over time they are not the same 'Angie' we met the first time due to their constant evolution, and perhaps, *changing identities* as a result of their everyday transition experiences. This also means that the transition support that worked for them yesterday might not work today.

In line with the Multiple and Multi-dimensional Transitions (MMT) Theory, discussed in detail later, your child's transitions will trigger transitions for you too. For example, you will also experience identity transitions due to your child's transitions. So does your identity as a parent change over time? Does it change from your perspective? Or does it change from the child's perspective? Something a lot of parents have mentioned is how their identities changed from the schools' perspectives, with them being seen as a primary school child's parent one day and a secondary school child's parent another day. No one has informed the parents of this change or what the rules of engagement are as a result of these different identities, but they are expected to navigate their own multiple transitions in different contexts along with supporting their child with their multiple transitions. This might seem similar to a thought experiment called the Ship of Theseus, which questions whether a ship which has had all its original components replaced over time is still the Ship of Theseus. The bigger question is whether it stopped being the Ship of Theseus once the first component was changed, or when the last one was changed?

WHAT ARE THE IMPLICATIONS OF PRIMARY-SECONDARY SCHOOL TRANSITIONS FOR OTHER EDUCATIONAL AND LIFE TRANSITIONS?

Unfortunately, there is little evidence of the impact of primary-secondary school transitions in the long term as studies only collect data at two time points, just before and after starting secondary school. Of the few, one mentioned earlier, West et al. (2010) found that children who had difficult transitions to secondary school did not stay to complete their schooling, with impact on their mental health and future employment chances.

Think of dominoes. One falls and it sets off a chain reaction. We can see the impact on the dominoes in front of us. What happens beyond that, when the dominoes are not in our line of vision? What happens when one ends up landing in a different way than expected or planned for? Professionals, especially primary school teachers, talk about not knowing how their student is doing in secondary school, despite most likely being in a similar location. Universities ask their students to complete leavers' destinations questionnaires with really low response rate. What about those children who didn't take a normative educational or employment route? However, if our focus is on children's emotional wellbeing, as can be seen from Chapters 2 and 3, the impact of primary-secondary school transitions on emotional wellbeing will impact every transition in their life at that moment in time, with repercussions to unresolved issues continuing to impact them in future, with potential for long-term mental health issues emerging.

FAMILIES AND FRIENDS AS STRONGEST SUPPORT NETWORKS

As transitions are ongoing, children will require ongoing support. The schools might have stopped providing the child explicit support for transitions, but parents might have to carry on providing support (see Vignette 1.4).

VIGNETTE 1.4. SUMMER HOLIDAYS BEFORE STARTING SECONDARY SCHOOL

Sammy has some questions about secondary school but there are no teachers around to ask them as the holidays have started. However, they are not daunted about that as they are getting support from their family. They told us:

> My family are doing really well to prepare me for moving to North High. They are making sure that I won't have any fears about going to the bigger school.
>
> They have told me what it would be like and how I would know where to go and I am thinking positively now about moving.

After starting secondary school

Sammy talked about how they were being supported when they started secondary school:

> My mum drove me to North High for the first week which helped me because I didn't really know the way to

school confidently. My brother who is in the older years of North High also walked in with me, so I wasn't alone.

Most importantly, they help me by just listening to me!

At dinner time they ask me how my day was and make me feel I can share my feelings and problems with them. That really helps me as I feel less stressed about things after that.

Our research has found that most children identify their parents/ grandparents, siblings and friends as their most important support networks, both for academic and personal issues (Jindal-Snape, 2018; Jindal-Snape & Cantali, 2019). This is perhaps not surprising as, like Alex and Sammy, they might have the most support needs during the times when professionals are not available. Further, their family, in particular, and to some extent their friends, will be their most consistent support network. In a world where everything might be changing around them, and that too at a rapid speed, having some known and trusted anchors like family members and friends are likely to help the child weather any potentially stormy seas. Also, just the presence of those anchors might make them confident about navigating these transitions, so they have less concerns about them from the start.

Therefore, it is important that parents talk with their children and encourage them to talk with others, such as siblings, classmates, friends and teachers, about what they are excited about, what they are worried about, and what strategies can they use to navigate transitions successfully. Parents sharing their own transitions experiences seemed to help children understand about transitions and secondary school.

For this to happen, however, parents need to be involved in the preparation and planning of their child's transitions by schools. They require clear and regular communications with the school. It is important that the focus is on '**with**' rather than it being a one-way street of schools giving, and deciding what information to give and

Figure 1.4 Talking about transitions with family.

Source: Jindal-Snape et al., 2023; Art: Clio Ding.

when. It requires **meaningful partnerships** (see Chapter 5 for more detail). Also, we need to be mindful that not every child might have support available from the family in this way and schools might need to provide extensive support (see Figure 1.4).

We will visit some of the aspects discussed here in more detail in the following chapters. Here we will conclude with some top tips from children and parents.

TOP TIPS FROM CHILDREN FOR CHILDREN

1. Talk to someone you know based in secondary school or your family.
2. Don't worry about things in secondary school. They will be better than you think. If you have a problem there are lots of people you can talk to.

Figure 1.5 Top tips.
Source: Jindal-Snape et al., 2023; Art: Clio Ding.

3. You will find the secondary school to be great and friendly. You will make new friends and have better opportunities.
4. It seems scary at the start but after two to three months it feels like you've always been there.
5. Try to figure out policies that happen in secondary school to prepare you before you move.

Some of the top tips have been summarised in Figure 1.5.

TOP TIPS FOR PARENTS FROM OTHER PARENTS

1. Have an ongoing conversation with the child and as a family about what transitions and successful transitions mean.
2. It is important to ask the child (on an ongoing basis) what they are excited about going to secondary school and what they are worried about. Follow it up with discussions of what the reality was after they started secondary school and over time.
3. Look out for any messages you or others in the environment might be giving to the child that might worry them. For example, even words like 'going up to the big school', although positive for some, can be worrying for others.
4. Bust any myths they might have heard about or negative discourses they might see in their environment, as soon as possible. However, consider doing this through a discussion as then the

child and you can explore the root of the discourse which might be more effective rather than asking them not to believe a message they are hearing repeatedly.

5. Discuss the strategies you or others you know used to navigate transitions to and through secondary school.

6. Discuss your own transitions as a result of the child's transitions.

7. Highlight the context of any questions or conversations. For example, instead of asking 'how are things?', maybe ask 'how are things at school' or 'how are things at the football club'?

8. Most importantly, remember the child is the expert about their transition experiences as are you of your own.

REFERENCES

Ashton, R. (2008). Improving the transfer to secondary school: How every child's voice can matter. *Support for Learning*, 23(4), 176–182.

Bagnall, C. L., Fox, C. L., & Skipper, Y. (2021). When is the 'optimal' time for school transition? An insight into provision in the US. *Pastoral Care in Education*, 39(4), 348–376.

Department for Education (2023). Number of schools for 'School characteristics' for Independent school, Non-maintained special school, State-funded AP school, State-funded nursery, State-funded primary and 2 other filters in England for 2023/24. Available from: https://explore-education-statistics.service.gov.uk/data-tables/permalink/24b3a94a-8bb6-41d0-1318-08dd12e09af5

Department for Education (2024). Annual Report. Available from: https://www.gov.uk/government/publications/department-for-education-consolidated-annual-report-and-accounts-2024-to-2025

Eccles, J. S., Midgley, C., Wigfield, A., Buchanan, C. M., Reuman, D., Flanagan, C., & Mac Iver, D. (1993). Development during adolescence: The impact of stage environment fit in young adolescents' experiences in schools and families. *American Psychologist*, 48, 90–101.

Evangelou, M., Taggart, B., Sylva, K., Melhuish, E., Sammons, P., & Siraj-Blatchford, I. (2008). *Effective Pre-school, Primary and Secondary Education 3–14 Project (EPPSE 3–14) What Makes a Successful Transition from Primary to Secondary School?* DCSF Publications.

Galton, M., Gray, J., & Ruddock, J. (2003). *Transfer and Transition in the Middle Years of Schooling (7–14): Continuities and Discontinuities in Learning*. Department for Education and Skills, Research Report RR443. DfES Publications.

Gutman, L. M., & Eccles, J. S. (2007). Stage–Environment fit during adolescence: Trajectories of family relations and adolescent outcomes. *Developmental Psychology*, 43(2), 522–537.

Jindal-Snape, D. (2016). *The A–Z of Transitions*. Palgrave Macmillan. https://doi.org/10.1057/978-1-137-52827-8

Jindal-Snape, D. (2018). Transitions from early years to primary and primary to secondary schools in Scotland. In T. Bryce, W. Humes, D. Gillies, & A. Kennedy (Eds.), *Scottish Education,* 5th edn. Edinburgh University Press, 281–292.

Jindal-Snape, D. (2023). Multiple and multi-dimensional educational and life transitions: Conceptualization, theorization and XII pillars of transitions. In R. J. Tierney, F. Rizvi, & K. Erkican (Eds.), *International Encyclopedia of Education (Fourth Edition)* (4th ed., pp. 530–543). Elsevier. https://doi.org/10.1016/B978-0-12-818630-5.14060-6

Jindal-Snape, D., Barlow, W., Goode, T., Hannah, E. F. S., Tooman, T., Ding, C., Burns, M., & Santiago, T. L. (2023a). *Multiple and Multi-dimensional Primary-Secondary School Transitions: Using Drama to Facilitate Transitions*. UniVerse. https://doi.org/10.20392/nx7a-bj66

Jindal-Snape, D., Bradshaw, P., Gilbert, A., Smith, N., & Knudsen, L. (2023b). Primary–secondary school transition experiences and factors associated with differences in these experiences: Analysis of the longitudinal Growing Up in Scotland dataset. *Review of Education*, 11(3), Article e3444. https://doi.org/10.1002/rev3.3444

Jindal-Snape, D., & Cantali, D. (2019). A four-stage longitudinal study exploring pupils' experiences, preparation and support systems during primary-secondary school transitions. *British Educational Research Journal*, 45(6), 1255–1278. https://doi.org/10.1002/berj.3561

Jindal-Snape, D., Hannah, E. F. S., Cantali, D., Barlow, W., & MacGillivray, S. (2020). Systematic literature review of primary-secondary transitions: International research. *Review of Education*, 8(2), 526–566. https://doi.org/10.1002/rev3.3197

Nguyen, T., Reynolds, K., & Klik, K. (2017). *School Structure and School Outcomes: Comparing Primary to High School Transitions in Traditional and P-10 Schools in the ACT*. Science at the Australian National University.

Pietarinen, J., Pyhältö, K., & Soini, T. (2010). A horizontal approach to school transitions: A lesson learned from Finnish 15-year-olds. *Cambridge Journal of Education*, 40(3), 229–245.

Scottish Government (2025). Independent schools in Scotland: Register. Available here: https://www.gov.scot/publications/independent-schools-in-scotland-register/

Symonds, J., & Hargreaves, L. (2016). Emotional and motivational engagement at school transition: A qualitative stage-environment fit study. *Journal of Early Adolescence*, 36(1), 54–85. https://doi.org/10.1177/0272431614556348

Symonds, J. E., Jindal-Snape, D., Bagnall, C., Hannah, B., & Barlow, B. (2024). School transitions in human and adolescent development. In L. Juang (Ed.), *Encyclopedia of Adolescence. Vol 2. Interpersonal and sociocultural factors* (2nd ed., pp. 434–446). Elsevier. https://doi.org/10.1016/

West, P., Sweeting, H. & Young, R. (2010) Transition matters: Pupils' experiences of the primary-secondary school transition in the West of Scotland and consequences for well-being and attainment. *Research Papers in Education*, 25(1), 21–50.

2

WHAT IS EMOTIONAL WELLBEING AND WHAT DO I NEED TO KNOW?

INTRODUCTION

In Chapter 1, we have discussed the impact of primary-secondary school transitions on children's "wellbeing", but what do we mean by this term? What does it include and not include? Are there different types of wellbeing, such as emotional wellbeing? And how does emotional wellbeing differ from mental health? Is this important? This chapter will address these questions, as well as some advice on what you could do to monitor and support children's emotional wellbeing, informed by research (including our own), which has drawn on the voices of children and those supporting them.

WHAT DOES THE TERM EMOTIONAL WELLBEING MEAN?

These questions are understandable, as over the last few years, there has been a dramatic focus on 'wellbeing', which has become a popular buzzword within the media, workplace and education, especially following the COVID-19 pandemic and the increase in poor wellbeing and poor mental health which followed. However, despite

DOI: 10.4324/9781032716145-2

being spoken about so frequently, there is lack of shared understanding of what we mean by the term 'wellbeing'. In fact, "wellbeing" as a concept is inconsistently defined, and several reviews of published journal articles have found no clear definitions of wellbeing (Jindal-Snape et al., 2014; Toma et al., 2014).

DEFINING WELLBEING

Let's start with an example; do any of the following sound familiar to you:

• "I have nothing to do, I am bored, I am so depressed"
"You are giving me anxiety, nagging about these chores"
"She is a psycho, running that much"

This is an example of how every day, normal emotions are being conflated, on a regular basis in everyday speech, with clinical mental health conditions, e.g., anxiety and depression; in addition to human behaviour conflated with a chronic mental health disorder, e.g., psychopathy.

This is not surprising as, you will know yourself, all of us use the term 'wellbeing' in very different ways. This might be due to how it is written about in literature, books that you or your child might read, how schools portray it and how it is represented in media. Of course, there are again differences in how wellbeing is defined based on whether you are a mental health nurse, psychologist or a teacher, and even yourself as a parent, all bringing our own learning at school, university, or work to talk about it. Therefore, some will see it as a tangible, objective concept, for instance, for a doctor it might be seen in the context of physical health, for a teacher as rights to adequate education and to an occupational health practitioner as life circumstances such as work-life balance. Some might place greater emphasis on the subjective aspects such as how my child feels when they are with friends and/or how they behave.

This is what we call the inter-disciplinary nature of wellbeing and means that the term has been used to describe our physical, social and emotional health. This book focusses on emotional wellbeing, which is a critical component of our health, including our mental health, and is especially important when considering primary-secondary school transitions. Emotional wellbeing is concerned with hedonia (e.g., positive and negative affect and life satisfaction; 'feeling well') and eudaimonia (e.g., welfare and functioning, 'doing well'), which we will discuss in more detail below using a worked example, as can be seen from Sammy's experience (see Vignette 2.1).

VIGNETTE 2.1. UNDERSTANDING SAMMY'S EMOTIONAL WELLBEING OVER PRIMARY-SECONDARY SCHOOL TRANSITIONS

In class, when Sammy's primary school teacher asked them to think about some of the changes they are likely to experience over primary-secondary school transitions, Sammy found themselves getting uncomfortably hot, feeling a bit sweaty and lost for words. This made Sammy feel worried and nervous about how they would manage these unexpected emotions at secondary school.

At break time, Sammy began reflecting on why their body had all of a sudden responded like this during class. Several of Sammy's friends from primary school were going to the same secondary school as them, which was reassuring, and Sammy always felt able to speak to their mum Jade about their worries. They were not sure why they had started to feel this way, as they had not started to think about secondary school yet and were unsure how they felt about the changes ahead, and how it would impact their everyday life in a few months' time.

What Sammy was feeling, were new emotions, that they had not experienced before, which is what several of the children within our research (Bagnall et al., 2024, 2025) have shared with us when we asked them to describe their emotional wellbeing when thinking about primary-secondary school transitions, which we will discuss later in this chapter. Concerning this chapter, in relation to emotional wellbeing, Sammy describes components of hedonia such as feeling "worried", including behavioural responses such as "sweating", but also managing these thoughts and emotions in relation to their welfare and functioning at secondary school, reflecting eudomonia.

As shown above Sammy's feelings of hedonia and eudomonia were not distinct, and overlapped, and together provide a comprehensive account of their emotional wellbeing. This has also been shown in research, with emotional wellbeing used as an umbrella label for understanding human feelings such as: positive and negative affect (e.g., moods, emotions, states); thoughts, such as sense of meaning and purpose (e.g., life satisfaction, social connection), and behaviours (e.g., feelings of autonomy, competence) (Khanna et al., 2024).

CHILDREN'S AND TEACHERS' DEFINITIONS OF EMOTIONAL WELLBEING

Children have described their own emotional wellbeing very similarly, in terms of their emotions (happy, joyful), thoughts (positive thinking), behaviours (smiling, laughing) and functioning (particularly of safety and stability) in our own and others research.

In our own research, primary-secondary school transitions-aged children described their emotional wellbeing as "how people feel, their emotions and their mental health". Children discussed their emotional wellbeing as the extent to which they feel "like their usual self" and can "think positive and not negative". Interestingly, children also defined their emotional wellbeing in line with their motivation and achieving what they have the capacity to achieve: "He is ready to learn, he is motivated like he's got…good standards". In addition, emotional wellbeing was defined as how comfortable the children felt in their social interactions: "I think positive wellbeing is like when you're happy…and…like if you're feeling comfortable around people", and how they treat others: "It means when you're like friendly and like you're saying positive stuff about them" (Bagnall et al., 2025, p. 19, 20 & 21).

In this same research, we also asked the children's teachers to describe what emotional wellbeing looks like in primary-secondary school transition-aged children (e.g.,Year 6 children in England and P7 children in Scotland [aged 10 and 11 years]).We have illustrated the protective factors discussed using an infographic in Figure 2.1.

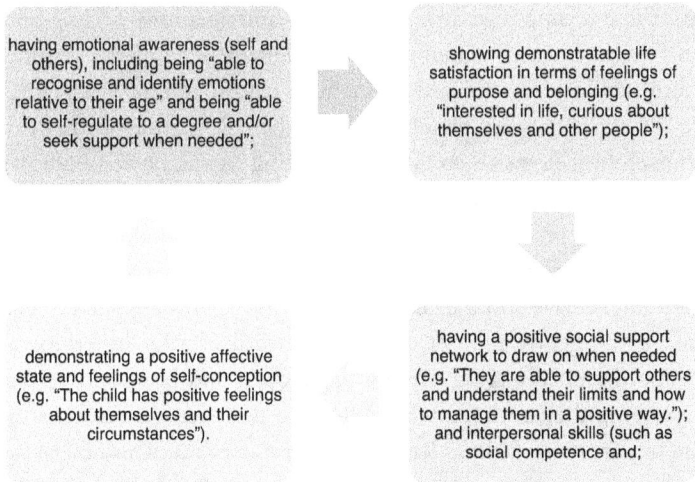

having emotional awareness (self and others), including being "able to recognise and identify emotions relative to their age" and being "able to self-regulate to a degree and/or seek support when needed";

showing demonstratable life satisfaction in terms of feelings of purpose and belonging (e.g. "interested in life, curious about themselves and other people");

demonstrating a positive affective state and feelings of self-conception (e.g. "The child has positive feelings about themselves and their circumstances").

having a positive social support network to draw on when needed (e.g. "They are able to support others and understand their limits and how to manage them in a positive way."); and interpersonal skills (such as social competence and;

Figure 2.1 Teacher's descriptions of what emotional wellbeing protective factors look like in primary-secondary school transfer-aged children.

What was found in this research, which is particularly interesting, and draws on the negative, deficit-oriented discourse which often underpins research surrounding mental health and primary-secondary school transitions (which will be discussed in Chapter 4) is the balanced discourse that practitioners and children used. An example is this quote by one of the teachers:

> A child with good emotional wellbeing will display the appropriate emotion in relation to the situation. Emotional wellbeing isn't always about being emotionally strong and positive, it is healthy for children to cry, feel sadness and frustration if a situation occurs that is likely to trigger such emotion.
>
> (Bagnall et al., 2025, p. 16 and 17)

This consideration has implications for yourself as a parent in supporting your child to identify, understand and manage their own and others emotional wellbeing in a balanced manner, recognising that it is normal to experience both positive and negative emotions, and that these feelings can be circumstantial and fleeting.

Thinking about Sammy's case (Vignette 2.1), Jade (Sammy's mum) could pick a relaxed moment to talk to Sammy – this might be a particular time during the day where it is more natural, and your child feels more conformable talking (it might be while your child is doing an activity, e.g., having a kickabout, doodling, baking). Giving children time to calm down can be helpful for more clear thinking, and it is likely that once Sammy has returned home, they might have had a chance to reflect on what happened in class. Jade could gently prompt discussions (see it as a bit like throwing a rope) by encouraging Sammy to be open and honest in verbally describing their feelings, where they can feel them in the body and the impact these feelings had on their frame of mind and behaviour at the time. In responding to Sammy, it is important that Jade shows empathy and compassion and encourages Sammy to recognise that no emotion is "wrong", and all feelings are valid and normal, and part of being human. Jade could share an example of how she has experienced similar feelings, thoughts and behaviours in relation to transitions experiences she has navigated (e.g., this could be moving house, changing jobs, becoming a mother), and how she managed them. This will make Jade more relatable to Sammy and normalise their feelings, which is important in nurturing trusting, empathetic parent-child relationships and in encouraging Sammy to continue sharing their experiences with Jade. This will also reassure Sammy that these emotions will pass, and what is important is learning how to manage them.

Crucial to similar interactions with your child is helping your child to recognise when they are feeling this way, understand that these feelings are normal and part of being human, and what they can do about this to change how they are feeling. Examples of inter-actions to support this learning could be modelling these behaviours yourself in everyday interactions at home and/or in the commu-nity, pointing out these behaviours in others in real-life or in games or on the television. It is also important to expose your child to some positive strategies to manage difficult emotions and practice them with your child in a safe-space, so they know how to use them when they arise in the future (e.g., breathing techniques, counting to ten slowly). As part of your discussions, it would be useful to help your child know how and when to ask for help from a safe adult (e.g., who could be a source of support in particular settings, such as school, in the community; the more the better) and the importance of doing so to keep themselves safe.

HOW DOES EMOTIONAL WELLBEING DIFFER FROM MENTAL HEALTH?

Mental health is like physical health but focusses on how we think, feel and behave. Everyone has mental health and like emotional wellbeing, it can range from good to poor and fluctuate temporarily (e.g., changes in mood, and/or energy levels throughout the day/week), or persis-tently when concerning more long-term mental health conditions. Good mental health might look like managing your daily life and the stresses that come with this well. It might look like having healthy rela-tionships, working well at school or at work, being able to cope with difficulties and adapt to changing circumstances. Poor mental health might impact the way someone is feeling, thinking or behaving, and cause them upset or problems. This might be in their relationships, at work or at school. Changes in mental health may be shaped by change in our resources (both personal and environmental factors), perspectives and experiences, which are aspects that you can look out for.

Like definitions of emotional wellbeing, there is also a lack of agreement about how to define 'mental health'. In fact, emotional wellbeing and mental health are commonly placed alongside each other, sometimes considered synonymous or otherwise rarely distinguished. To help with this, we have provided some information below about what mental health conditions look like, and Lucy's case (see Vignette 2.2), who has sadly struggled with her mental health for some time.

MENTAL HEALTH CONDITIONS

Mental-ill health conditions are believed to be caused by an interaction between our biology, genes and individual make-up, in addition to our environment, including family background, society and life experiences, which is referred to in psychology as the Diathesis-Stress Model. The Diathesis-Stress Model offers a theory for how psychological disorders emerge by considering the interacting impact of vulnerability (diathesis) and stress, recognising that not all diatheses are created equal, and therefore have a differing impact on the likelihood of developing a mental illness, which is referred to by Theadore as the "cup analogy" (See Scenario 2.2):

SCENARIO 2.2. CUP ANALOGY

Imagine several cups filled with different amounts of marbles; when water is poured into those cups, the cups with more marbles will overflow more easily. Diatheses are like marbles, and stress is like water: the greater the diathesis, the less stress is needed to cause "overflow" (i.e., give rise to mental illness)

One important distinction between emotional wellbeing and mental health is that mental health difficulties can be recognised and diagnosed, by a GP (e.g., for more common problems such as depression and anxiety) or a mental-health specialist, following The Diagnostic and Statistical Manual of Mental Disorders.

Mental health conditions are not 'passing' feelings but are more long-lasting, debilitating and have an impact on the child's day-to-day life. To understand this, see if you can identify between the primary disturbance in mood and emotion in response to a given stressor Sammy (Vignette 2.1) was experiencing relating to primary-secondary school transitions, and Lucy's (Vignette 2.3) debilitating symptoms.

VIGNETTE 2.3. UNDERSTANDING LUCY'S MENTAL HEALTH

Lucy has been experiencing mental ill-health difficulties since she lost her younger sister one year ago. At first, Lucy showed somatic complaints such as frequent stomachaches throughout the day, had no energy and felt tired all the time. Lucy used to play with her friends most days after school outside at the park, but was no longer interested in this, and became very withdrawn, spending large periods of time in bed, under the covers where it was darker, but despite feeling tired couldn't sleep.

Lucy's teacher, Rebecca, at school noticed that Lucy's behaviour had changed; she had little appetite at lunch or breaktime and was no longer interacting with her peers. She preferred to sit by herself in class and had lost interest towards her schoolwork, often looking very tired. Rebecca spoke to Lucy's mum (Stacey), who encouraged Lucy to speak to the school counsellor, who referred Lucy to Child and Adolescent Mental Health Services (CAMHS).

Lucy was diagnosed with depression, and began to get help in identifying, understanding and managing her symptoms. After six months of weekly counselling and family therapy,

Lucy began to feel much better, and Stacey (Lucy's mum) noticed that she was getting her Lucy back. From working with CAMHS, as well as Rebecca (Lucy's teacher), Stacey felt more confident in knowing the signs to look out for at home and school, to monitor her mental health and felt reassured knowing that others were looking out for Lucy too and knew her history.

Next year Lucy will be moving to secondary school, and Stacey and Rebecca have already started discussions with her Year 7 form tutor, Simon, to ensure that the same co-ordinated approach will be in place to support Lucy when she starts secondary school.

As can be seen from Vignettes 2.1 to 2.3, a child struggling with their emotional wellbeing may exhibit symptoms of poor mental-ill health, such as somatic complaints (e.g., a stomachache, feeling tired) and may show withdrawn behaviours (e.g., preferring to be on their own, sleeping more often). However, several of these symptoms collectively may fall under the DSM criteria for diagnosing a mental health disorder, which is when a problem is particularly severe or persistent over time, or when a number of these difficulties are experienced at the same time, as shown in Lucy's case.

You could think about emotional wellbeing like a see-saw, or quite simply a balance point between our available resources and the challenges/changes we are facing. Each time we face challenges/changes, our resources (e.g., support from others, coping skills and beliefs) come into a state of imbalance, and we need to adapt to get back to equilibrium. Adapting to changing and difficult circumstances, while keeping mentally healthy, enables us to expand what we call in psychology "our window of tolerance", in other words our *resilience,* which has been defined as: "the ability to bend, but not break, bounce back and perhaps even grow in the face of adverse life experience" (Southwick et al., 2014); 'difficulty', 'stress' or 'adversity' being central to the concept of resilience, as is positive adaptation. Resilience literature aims to understand what protective and risk factors within ourselves (e.g., this could be coping skills) and our environments (e.g., supportive relationships) impact our emotional wellbeing.

You can support the development of your child's resilience by helping them to identify when they are experiencing a changing and difficult circumstance, which they are finding stressful and/or emotionally challenging, what emotional responses to look out for and what they can do to manage their feelings by drawing on protective factors (e.g., ask for help from a safe adult, use their problem-solving and coping skills). It is important that your child knows that doing so will reduce the impact of the changing and difficult circumstance on their emotional wellbeing, and subsequent mental-ill health.

Critical periods, such as school transitions, where children are more likely to experience social, academic, environmental, and personal changes and challenges (to name a few), can be a disruptive time. It can lead to a dip in this see-saw, if sufficient support is not in place, e.g., social support from parents, peers and teachers, development of positive coping skills and beliefs through emotional-centred support interventions. Therefore, as parents, focus should be placed on helping to manage children's expectations during transitions, to support your child's resilience in being able to adapt to these changes.

You could do this by gradually developing children's transition knowledge, awareness and skills to manage the multiple changes they will experience over primary-secondary school transitions (which will be discussed in further detail in Chapter 5). This could be through "testing-out" transitions skills within similar scenarios and encouraging children to draw on available social support. An example of a transitions skill which you could model and practice with your child is asking for help from a "safe stranger" in the supermarket, e.g., by encouraging your child to ask a supermarket assistant where the "eggs" are in the supermarket. Another could be encouraging your child to make some choices and decisions for themselves, and scaffolding skills to doing this, e.g., supporting your child to manage their time, wake themselves up in the morning.

MENTAL HEALTH LITERACY

From a practical perspective, distinctions between emotional wellbeing and mental health can be important. Mental health conditions can be difficult to talk about and are often poorly misunderstood, and emotional wellbeing is perceived as less threatening, and as a result accessing support for emotional wellbeing is favoured and perceived as less stigmatising.

This is concerning, as 1 in 5 children in the UK (DfE, 2023), have a probable mental health disorder (an increase from 1 in 9 in 2017 to 1 in 6 in 2022), yet only 60% of children access mental health and wellbeing support. Thus, recognising that numbers of children experiencing mental health complaints is increasing rapidly, especially long-term mental health conditions, prevention and early intervention of mental health problems is paramount, as shown in Vignette 2.2, and greater early-intervention focus on emotional wellbeing can support this.

As also illustrated in Vignette 2.2, education services are the most reported source of help and advice for children with mental health concerns and their parents. Recognising this, there has been a surge in recent years in delivery of mental health literacy interventions (Foulkes & Stapley, 2022), which have been shown to increase children's:

1. mental health and emotional awareness in themselves and others (e.g., empathy);
2. development of internal and external positive coping strategies
3. strengths to build insight and confidence in their abilities (e.g., keeping well), resilience and to avoid rumination.

Programmes do this by focussing on the language used, steering away from exploring specific mental health difficulties, and instead focus on recognising common emotions as normal within different contexts (e.g., over primary-secondary school transitions, worry can be a normal but fleeting emotion).

This sense of universality to mental health has been reflected in a recent research study (Hosking et al., 2024), which explored children's experiences and feelings towards primary-secondary school transitions, following participating in a mental health literacy intervention, in the final year of primary school. For example, further corroborating the see-saw analogy, in addition to the universality of mental health, one child said:

> mental health is in every human being and like you can't just say I don't want it...like there are times when things are harder but like it can change, we can bounce between feeling like things are okay to um then not. Like my mental health isn't poor, as I'm not worried, but it's knowing what I do that keeps me feeling well, that's important.
>
> (Hosking et al., 2024, p. 113)

There was also an overall sense of the children "being present" and "in the moment" with their concerns about primary-secondary school transitions, and the mental health literacy curriculum was also shown to help children perceive their worries as fleeting, normal and manageable: "I'll probably feel butterflies in my stomach, but I will only feel that when I first go there" (Hosking et al., 2024,. 106).

These findings demonstrate the importance of contextualising learning about mental health and have implications for yourselves as parents in terms of ensuring discussions about mental health are sensitive, child-led and align with a balanced discourse. This is especially reflecting the fact that Hosking et al.'s (2024) research found that previous exposure to different messages and misinformation around mental health can cause confusion and the overall picture of mental health as something to fear in themselves and others. This can have harmful implications, with regard to downplaying or internalising worries due to fears of being judged and stigmatised. There are also concerns that mental health literacy programmes can increase over-identification and labelling normal emotional responses, if not supported sensitively.

Therefore, it is important that as parents, we are mindful of the language that we use, and the mental health messages that we expose our child to (e.g., the media, television programmes). As we will discuss in Chapter 4 as parents and practitioners, we should be mindful that the discourse we use when talking about emotional wellbeing and mental health is positive, follows a strengths-based approach, to create environments and opportunities to empower children and increase their confidence in recognising mental health as nothing to be afraid of. It is important that parents establish a safe space, for children to feel comfortable discussing mental health in themselves and/or others, and scaffold supportive, child-led conversations. Focus should be placed on helping children to normalise their worries without making it seem trivial (e.g., we all get worried sometimes, but I know that can feel hard, make you feel uncomfortable and overwhelmed, which can be difficult to manage), increase their understanding and confidence in being able to identify positive and negative emotions in themselves and others (e.g., you could model this, which will reducing fear and stigma surrounding mental health), and what your child should do when they feel this way, to help feel more comfortable (e.g., seek support from a safe adult, use learnt problem-solving skills).

An example of a school setting which got this right was shown in our case study research within a special school (Bagnall et al., 2021), that specialised in supporting children with social, emotional and mental health (SEMH) difficulties. From speaking to both children, and staff within the school, it was clear that a safe, supportive environment had been established within the school, which normalised open discussion towards emotional literacy (e.g., emotional awareness, understanding and regulation), which meant that children were able to identify their feelings, freely discuss their emotions and thought-processes and access support for themselves and others. While it is worth noting that the children's open discussion of mental health literacy may also be indicative of the additional awareness and support children receive in special schools; understanding more widely the mechanisms through which special schools facilitate a more open approach to mental health has useful implications for mental health literacy provisions in mainstream schools for both staff and students, and what you can do as parents to model similar approaches at home.

In the special school, children are taught in small class sizes of no more than ten children, staffed by a teacher and a teaching assistant. Such intimate settings, which combine features of a standard classroom with a family-type setting, can help better meet the needs of children with SEMH difficulties, especially when concerning emotional security and positive engagement. Safe, nurturing settings can also help to position emotional wellbeing at the heart of school practice, which should be a priority in all primary and secondary schools.

One strategy, the school used to support children's mental health literacy was "feelings balls" which were used to help the children to identify when they were struggling with their emotions, and signpost these feelings to their class teacher, that they needed some support (see Figure 2.2). Making similar feelings balls could be a shared craft activity that you as parents could do at home with your child, to continue mental health literacy discussions that your child will be having in school. This would form a more applied activity and provide a visual in setting up a 'safe space' with your child, and help to consolidate your child's learning in class, generalise this learning to the home and promote an openness to mental health discussions. Some useful discussion topics could be "what do we mean by mental health", "how would we know that a friend was struggling with their mental health", "how can we look after our mental health" and "what is the difference between emotional wellbeing and mental health".

Figure 2.2 "Feelings balls" used within a special primary school, to support children with social, emotional and mental health difficulties to identify when they were struggling with their emotions, and signpost these feelings to their class teacher, that they needed some support.

It is important that these discussions are child-led, sensitive, underpinned by a positive discourse, and scaffolded by empathy and a common understanding that there are no right and wrong emotions. To support these discussions, you could draw on some of the advice and strategies that we have discussed within this chapter, to increase your own and child's confidence in talking about emotional wellbeing, mental health and resilience, and to understand and identify positive and negative mental health in yourself and others. You might want to ask your child's teacher when your child will be having mental health literacy lessons within class (so that you can check-in with your child and follow-up at home), and what their curriculum looks like (so that you can target specific discussions to what might be covered in class). It might be that your child's school has home-learning activities which you could follow-up directly on.

HOW CAN A TEACHER MEASURE CHILDREN'S EMOTIONAL WELLBEING?

As discussed in this chapter, emotional wellbeing as a concept is poorly defined, understood, and as a result is often conflated with clinical mental health conditions, e.g., anxiety and depression, which as we know hold different meanings. It is also important to make you aware that most of the research on defining emotional wellbeing has been focussed on adults, and only recently has attention turned to understanding what emotional wellbeing means to children, and looks like in children, which we have shared with you above.

The same can be said when considering the next step in the chain, which is how we should go about measuring emotional wellbeing in children, and unsurprisingly there is no 'one size fits all' approach. In other words, emotional wellbeing is measured in different ways by different professionals. For example, doctors might use heart ratings and/or neuroimaging, whereas teachers might use observations of behaviour in class and break time, and an educational psychologist might use self-report (questionnaires completed by the individual about themselves) from children, and proxy reports from significant others, including teachers and parents. Within these different approaches, emphasis is often placed on the different components of emotional wellbeing, discussed earlier in the chapter.

Developmental research has shown that from the age of seven years, children are able to evaluate their feelings and experience of different emotions. There are increasing concerns about the mental health of young people, with recent evidence finding that 70% of children and adolescents who experience mental health problems have not had appropriate interventions at a sufficiently early age (DfE, 2023). Responding to this, it is common, and good practice, for schools to monitor pupils' emotional wellbeing, using well-established self-report questionnaires, at specific time points during the school year. Schools can then take a preventative approach in supporting children's mental health, by using cohort, group and individual scores to improve practice and support around mental health literacy and emotional wellbeing interventions. This is a significant public health issue, and a policy priority, as shown in the Department for Education's report (2021) "Whole School or College approach to Mental Health and Wellbeing", and the introduction of emotional health objectives within primary and secondary school OFSTED reports (monitors standards in schools, in England).

For example, in the case of Lucy (Vignette 2.2), Rebecca (Lucy's class teacher) could have identified that (1) Lucy was experiencing symptoms of low mood, through monitoring changes in her emotional wellbeing scores over time; (2) understand Lucy's strengths and needs across different aspects of emotional wellbeing, e.g., positive/negative emotions, self-esteem, to support referrals to school counsellors and/or CAMHS; (3) identify interventions which could be useful on both a targeted 1:1 and/or universal, whole-class basis to address identified needs (and allocate appropriate resourcing), and (4) evaluate their effectiveness (e.g., how their needs change over time, in response to additional support).

This information can also be used to identify patterns and trends across different school groups, or demographics, and create benchmarks to compare findings over time and inform school development plans. This model has been shown to be effective across primary and secondary schools within the Education Learning Trust in Stockport to support a contiguous approach to primary-secondary school transitions support provision (See Scenario 2.4).

SCENARIO 2.4. A CONTINUOUS APPROACH TO PRIMARY-SECONDARY SCHOOL TRANSITIONS SUPPORT PROVISION

"At the Education Learning Trust, we have developed a 13-week transition curriculum which spans the final period of Year 6 in feeder primary schools and the initial half term of Year 7 in secondary school. As part of this curriculum, we use pupil focus groups and surveys, including the CORC Wellbeing Measurement for Schools modular surveys, and the *Primary-Secondary School Transitions Emotional Wellbeing Scale (#P-S WELLS)* at selected time points (pre-programme, end of year six, start of year seven and post-programme) to measure how pupils confidence and wellbeing changed over this period. Initial data collected was hugely influential in how we were able to adapt to children's needs; be agile in approach to future sessions; and allowed us to share pertinent information with key adults in both settings. It was clear that this approach allowed us to focus more acutely on experiences that had the potential to positively impact the children's confidence and wellbeing rather than rigidly follow a set pathway of experiences and emerging data suggests that this monitoring is positively impacting on outcomes. However, this model did not effectively capture data on the emotional wellbeing of the parents in relation to this period and work now centres on developing two further layers of pupil/adult and separate adult only experiences which will support parents navigating the changes but also provide essential data collection opportunities for the study of how parent's emotion wellbeing tracks during this time" (Gary Wilson, Schools Partnership Coordinator, Educational Learning Trust).

HOW CAN A PARENT MONITOR THEIR CHILD'S EMOTIONAL WELLBEING AND FOLLOW UP WORK DONE IN CLASS?

First, it is important to mention that when responding to emotional wellbeing questions, the process of completing the questionnaire/s, itself guides pupils in thinking about their thoughts, feelings and behaviours, and how they are related. This can facilitate positive reflective processes amongst children, and help-seeking behaviour (Demkowicz et al., 2020). Completing questionnaires focussed on emotional wellbeing, in class alongside their classmates, as part of routine assessment and monitoring of a whole-school approach to mental health can be powerful in exemplifying to children that their school values their emotional wellbeing greatly and is committed to learning more about how they are feeling, and creating a positive learning environment, which can help pupils feel valued, and empowered.

Completing questionnaires alongside their peers can also send positive messages to children about the universality of mental health and emotional wellbeing, and normality of identifying positive and negative emotions. This can help to reduce fear and stigma surrounding mental health, and promote acceptability in talking about emotional wellbeing, to manage and improve it.

As parents, it is important to continue these open conversations at home, and in the community, which can help build trusting and empathetic relationships, and we have listed some strategies below.

It could be helpful and good practice for schools to notify parents, when children will be completing questionnaires in class about their emotional wellbeing, as parents can be mindful of this at home, and sensitively be there to provide follow-up support for their child. In the case of Sammy, Jade could have sensitively spoken to Sammy at home about what happened in class, when their teacher began talking about some of the changes they are likely to experience over primary-secondary school transitions, using some of the strategies discussed in Chapter 5.

WHAT CAN A PARENT DO TO SUPPORT THEIR CHILD'S EMOTIONAL WELLBEING?

Parents are the most significant and consistent support figures in children's lives, and have the most long-lasting influence. Parent support is shown to be directly related to children's academic success, self-esteem, confidence and overall psychological wellbeing than any other support figure (Jindal-Snape et al., 2020). This is unsurprising as parents play a central role in helping children to understand and manage their emotions in themselves and others. Parents provide a "secure base" for their children, and a crucial sense of safety and belonging, and are often the first-person children turn to when they are struggling, but also when things are difficult who are at the receiving-end of children's difficult emotions and behaviours; as children often take out their most difficult emotions on those closest to them. Thus, knowing how to best: (1) talk to children about their emotional wellbeing; (2) spot signs that children might be struggling with their emotional wellbeing and (3) look after your own emotional wellbeing while supporting children is important, and we have listed some strategies below under each subheading.

KNOWING HOW TO BEST TALK TO YOUR CHILD ABOUT THEIR EMOTIONAL WELLBEING

It is common as a parent to be concerned about how to best encourage and guide your child to talk about their emotional wellbeing, especially as children are transitioning into adolescence, navigating biological and hormonal changes associated with puberty, and children's attention becomes a lot more focussed on peer relationships. Because of this establishing supportive parent-child relationships early on in children's development can be important for building stable trusting and empathetic relationships throughout the life-course, as can encouraging and guiding your child to think about their mental health and wellbeing as an important component of their overall health.

To do this, it is important that your child knows that you are interested in their life and what is important to them, whether that is a school play, their football match and/or a television series that they are watching. Support and encourage your child's interests. This will also build a common ground between you and your child and let them know that you value them for who they are but will also provide natural and regular opportunities for you to check-in with your child about how they are feeling, reinforcing this open and safe sharing environment between yourself and your child, where their concerns are taken seriously and listened to.

Within these conversations, it is important to make sure that your child feels safe, has a sense of belonging and that you are there to listen, and want to listen, with the conversation led by your child. Providing opportunities to be present and connect with your child every day on a 1:1 basis can provide a foundation to start conversations about their emotional wellbeing. This will help to build trust, security and provide continuity in knowing that there is a designated space and time, where they feel comfortable to express how their day has gone and how they are feeling. This can help your child get used to talking about their feelings, and know that you are there to listen, and value this 1:1 time together. It can also make it easier for you, as a parent, to spot when you child may be struggling with a problem on their own and how to support them, such as in the case of Lucy.

When your child is talking to you as a parent, it is important to actively and empathetically listen to what they are saying, how they are saying it and how they are feeling, before responding. Pay attention to your child's body language, facial expressions and behaviour when they are talking, to try and understand how they are feeling, and how this is impacting their ability to function. This will help identify the scale of the problem, and how you can best support them in the moment but also on a day-to-day basis. We know it will be tempting to want to respond and 'fix' everything straightaway but try to focus at first on really listening and providing emotional support to your child. This will reassure your child and let them know that you are taking care to really understand their feelings and are listening to what they are saying seriously.

When you do respond, thank your child for sharing how they are feeling and be encouraging about the way they have opened up in a healthy and mature way. Let your child know that you love them, are there for them, and that they can talk to you whenever they need to, and you can help them get support if they need it and is relevant to the context. As part of this, spend some time together thinking about what is making your child feel this way, by talking through their feelings, thoughts and behaviours and how they might be interacting, in a calm and an age-appropriate manner. Try to see your child's concern through their eyes to get a real idea about their specific thoughts and feelings, stay calm and try to empathise with how it feels for them, and the importance to them in telling you. This creates an open and safe environment where children feel comfortable speaking about their mental health and emotional wellbeing.

When talking to your child, openly consider strategies with your child to help them to understand how they could resolve their situation. This will help to empower your child, foster their self-esteem and confidence in their own autonomy and competence in making healthy choices. Try to follow up with your child the next day and praise them for the way they have handled the situation and/or talk through what they could have done differently next time.

SPOTTING SIGNS THAT YOUR CHILD MIGHT BE STRUGGLING WITH THEIR EMOTIONAL WELLBEING

It is common for children to experience emotional difficulty from time-to-time, especially during critical periods, such as primary-secondary school transitions, where children are more likely to experience simultaneous change and challenge. However, spotting signs that your child might be struggling with their emotional wellbeing, when there hasn't been a specific event or immediate changes in their life, can be more difficult. To support you as parents, we have listed some potential things and patterns to look out for, which could indicate that your child might be struggling with their emotional wellbeing and might need some support.

Difficulties sleeping and changes in appetite. Although not all, some children like routine, which provides structure to their day, and helps them to feel a sense of security and stability. Try to build positive routines, such as healthy eating, regular exercise, and a good night's sleep. Keep to these regular routines, e.g., regular mealtimes, fixed times for going to bed and waking up, which can help identify signs that your child is upset, as somatic complaints (physical signs of difficulty) are often a first sign that they are struggling.

Not wanting to do things they usually like. You know your child better than anyone, so if you're worried, think if there could have been a significant event, or something someone has said/done, at home or at school, or at a club, which might be impacting changes in your child's behaviour in not wanting to engage in their hobby. This is where contextualising your child's feelings might be helpful, which is discussed in "changes in their behaviour" below.

Changes in their social interactions (especially withdrawing from social situations with peers). A key sign of children struggling with their emotional wellbeing can be when their relationships with their friends change; to help spot this, try to get to know the names of your child's friends and the dynamics of their relationships. Be attentive to any changes in the way your child talks about their friends, who they are playing with and their body language during interactions.

Changes in their behaviour. To understand changes in your child's mood and behaviour, it might be helpful to try and contextualise your child's feelings, to try and understand, for example, if your child is showing signs of being upset when coming home from school, or when going to school; after playing with friends online and/or in-person after school; following spending time on their own.

Neglecting themselves. A key sign of children struggling with their emotional wellbeing can be signs that they are not looking after themselves, e.g., not taking regular baths/showers, not brushing their hair and/or teeth, tidying their room. This might indicate that things are getting too much for your child, and they are struggling to manage with difficult feelings or experiences, and don't have the energy. Remember that being active, creative, learning new things and building social connections with others, can support children's emotional wellbeing; if your child is withdrawing from activities which use these skills, it might be a sign that they are struggling, and don't have the same energy as they used to have.

Once you have spotted signs that your child might be struggling with their emotional wellbeing, it is important that you try to talk to your child about this, in a calm and age-appropriate manner, and spend some time together thinking about what is making your child feel this way. Letting your child know that you have noticed these changes and want to be there for them and support them to feel better, may help to validate their feelings, and let them know that they are not the only ones that have noticed that they are feeling this way. This may also let your child know that you are looking out for them, because you love them, and care about their emotional wellbeing. Remind your child that their feelings are temporary, reassure them that things can change, and they can feel better. This will help to create an open, stable and safe base, where your child feels comfortable talking to you about how they are feeling. Ask your child if there is anything that you could do to support them that they would find particularly helpful, and that you will look out for them. Pay attention to the language that your child uses to describe their feelings, so that you can reflect on the terms that they use in your own language in the future. This will help them feel listened to and make what you say relatable.

It might be that your child is not ready to talk to you about how they are feeling; it might be helpful to think about it like you are throwing a rope out to see if it is the right moment for your child to catch the rope, sometimes they will be ready to catch the rope and talk, and sometimes they may not be ready, and it may take more time for your child to open up to you. If your child does not want to talk, this can feel difficult as a parent, but it is important to remember that it is not your fault, it is just that your child might not be ready to catch the rope yet. Try not to step back, and instead let your child know that you are there for them visibly (e.g., around the house, watching your child doing something they enjoy), and also provide them with resources to get information they may need elsewhere (e.g., another safe adult, a book, video and/or website which might be useful). This may make catching the rope easier for your child, once they are ready.

LOOKING AFTER YOUR OWN EMOTIONAL WELLBEING WHILE SUPPORTING YOUR CHILD

Being a parent is not an easy job, especially as children grow older and begin to make their own decisions. It can be hard supporting a child who is struggling with their emotional wellbeing, or if their mood and behaviour seem different, especially if you are not sure why or what you can do to help. It is completely normal to be worried about your child, and feel helpless, and feeling this way is nothing to be ashamed of; don't be hard on yourself, as you are not alone.

First, try to recognise and acknowledge when you are feeling overwhelmed. It is important that you talk to someone that you trust about how you are feeling and see what they think, and if they can help. Reach out to family and friends, who could support you and your child, and help you to take some time out for yourself to manage how you are feeling. Sometimes taking a step-back for an hour or so, to support yourself, and look after your own emotional wellbeing, will help you to better support your child's.

It can be upsetting and worrying if your child is struggling, and it can make your relationship with them feel more stressful, as children often take it out on those closest to them. This can be hard and seeking help is not an admission of guilt, but 'role-modelling' good mental health for our children.

To help feel less alone, many parents find it reassuring to meet other parents experiencing similar concerns or worries and share their experiences with each other through support groups. It might be helpful to talk to your child's school, who might know of some local and region-specific organisations and support groups which could help, and who could also look out for you and your child. There is also lots of online support available that has been specifically designed for parents.

TOP TIPS FROM CHILDREN FOR CHILDREN

1. It is important and healthy to talk to a safe adult about your thoughts and feelings, and how this can impact how you behave.

2. We all have mental health, it is nothing to be scared of; poor mental health is just like breaking a bone, we just need to get help.
3. It is important to know that everyone feels upset and worried at times. When people are down on themselves, don't judge them and instead try to help them to talk to a safe adult.
4. When you are worried, it is good to find things to take your mind off that feeling by doing something that you enjoy, such as playing with friends, doing a sports activity, a craft, baking (to name a few).

TOP TIPS FROM PARENTS FOR PARENTS

1. Provide opportunities to be present and connect with your child every day on a 1:1 basis to help them get used to talking about their feelings, using some of the strategies discussed above, and know that there is always someone there to listen.
2. Be mindful of the language you use to talk about emotional wellbeing and mental health, and pay attention to the language your child uses, so that you can use this language in your discussions.
3. Actively listen to and validate your child's feelings, and help your child to understand, identify and manage their emotions in constructive ways.
4. Pay attention to any changes in your child's mood and behaviour, this might be a sign that they are struggling with their emotional wellbeing.
5. It is important to look after your own emotional wellbeing while supporting your child's emotional wellbeing.

REFERENCES

Bagnall, C. L., Fox, C. L., & Skipper, Y. (2021). What emotional-centred challenges do children attending special schools face over primary–secondary school transition? *Journal of Research in Special Educational Needs*, 21(2), 156–167. https://doi.org/10.1111/1471-3802.12507

Bagnall, C. L., Jindal-Snape, D., Panayiotou, M., & Qualter, P. (2024). Design and validation of the primary-secondary school transitions emotional wellbeing scale (PS WELLS); the first scale to assess children's emotional wellbeing in the context of primary-secondary school transitions. *International Journal of Educational and Life Transitions*, 3(1), 4. https://doi.org/10.5334/ijelt.79

Bagnall, C.L., Jindal-Snape, D., Panayiotou, M., Qualter, P., Banwell, E., & Mason, C. (2025). Emotional wellbeing in the context of primary-secondary school transitions: A concept analysis. *Educational Psychology Review*, 37, 21. https://doi.org/10.1007/s10648-025-09990-6.

Demkowicz, O., Ashworth, E., Mansfield, R., Stapley, E., Miles, H., Hayes, D., … & Deighton, J. (2020). Children and young people's experiences of completing mental health and wellbeing measures for research: Learning from two school-based pilot projects. *Child and Adolescent Psychiatry and Mental Health*, 14, 1–18. https://doi.org/10.1186/s13034-020-00341-7

Department for Education (2021). *Promoting children and young people's mental health and wellbeing: A whole school or college approach*. Available from https://assets.publishing.service.gov.uk/media/614cc965d3bf7f718518029c/Promoting_children_and_young_people_s_mental_health_and_wellbeing.pdf

Department for Education (2023). *State of the nation: Children and young people's wellbeing*. Available from: https://www.gov.uk/government/collections/state-of-the-nation-reports-children-and-young-peoples-wellbeing

Foulkes, L., & Stapley, E. (2022). Want to improve school mental health interventions? Ask young people what they actually think. *Journal of Philosophy of Education*, 56(1), 41–50. https://doi.org/10.1111/1467-9752.12649

Hosking, A. C. (2024). Mental Health and Resilience Sessions and How They Support Transition from Primary to Secondary School: Exploring Young Peoples' Experiences to Inform Further Development and Research (DClin Thesis)

Jindal-Snape, D., Hannah, E. F. S., Cantali, D., Barlow, W., & MacGillivray, S. (2020). Systematic literature review of primary-secondary transitions: International research. *Review of Education*, 8(2), 526–566. https://doi.org/10.1002/rev3.3197

Jindal-Snape, D., Scott, R., & Davies, D. (2014). 'Arts and smarts': assessing the impact of arts participation on academic performance during school years. Systematic literature review (Work package 2).

Khanna, D., Black, L., Panayiotou, M., Humphrey, N., & Demkowicz, O. (2024). Conceptualising and measuring adolescents' hedonic and eudemonic wellbeing: Discriminant validity and dimensionality concerns. *Child Indicators Research*, 17(2), 551–579. https://doi.org/10.1007/s12187-024-10106-9

Southwick, S. M., Bonanno, G. A., Masten, A. S., Panter-Brick, C., & Yehuda, R. (2014). Resilience definitions, theory, and challenges: interdisciplinary perspectives. *European Journal of Psychotraumatology*, 5(1), 25338. https://doi.org/10.3402/ejpt.v5.25338

Toma, M., Morris, J., Kelly, C., & Jindal-Snape, D. (2014). The impact of art attendance and participation on health and wellbeing: systematic literature review (work package 1).

3

———————

WHY IS IT IMPORTANT TO UNDERSTAND CHILDREN'S EMOTIONAL WELLBEING DURING PRIMARY-SECONDARY SCHOOL TRANSITIONS?

INTRODUCTION

Pulling together our reading from Chapters 1 and 2, in this chapter we will focus on why it is important to understand children's emotional wellbeing during primary-secondary school transitions. As part of this, we will discuss what emotional wellbeing "means" in the context of primary-secondary school transitions, and why this understanding is important for yourself as a parent in how you understand and know about your child's experiences during this time, to support them.

WHY IS IT IMPORTANT TO FOCUS ON EMOTIONAL WELLBEING DURING PRIMARY-SECONDARY SCHOOL TRANSITIONS?

As outlined in Chapter 1, primary-secondary school transitions can be emotionally demanding, ongoing periods for children

DOI: 10.4324/9781032716145-3

and yourselves as parents. Children and parents have highlighted this in our research (Bagnall et al., 2024a; Jindal-Snape & Cantali, 2019), as have teachers (Bagnall et al., 2020), and policymakers (DfE, 2023). This is unsurprising when we think about the multiple and simultaneous changes, or resultant "transitions" that you and your child navigate during this time (see Chapters 1 and 7, Jindal-Snape's Multiple and Multi-dimensional Transitions Theory (MMT, 2016, 2023)).

These transitions span across multiple domains (e.g., psychological, educational, social) and contexts (e.g., school, home, community). Primary-secondary school transitions are also nested amongst other developmental transitions, such as hormonal changes associated with puberty (Ng-Knight et al., 2016), in addition to school-based pressures, such as academic national Standard Assessment Tests in England, which can cause feelings of emotional instability.

As discussed in Chapter 2, managing multiple changes simultaneously, within a short period of time, can impact children's ability to cope, and their emotional wellbeing. For example, whereas ourselves as adults, see the "major life event" of transferring to a new school as more significant, for children, the "daily hassles", or transitions challenges inherent within this, such as getting lost, having a disagreement with a classmate, asking for help (to name a few) are perceived as more difficult, and many children report feelings of stress and anxiety during this time (Jindal-Snape & Miller, 2008; White, 2020).

Similar to the scenario in Chapter 1 about Sammy and multiple balls being thrown at them, the Strength Model of Self-Control (Baumeister et al., 2007) outlines how an individual's ability to cope deteriorates as the number of stressors in their life accumulates, co-exists and persists. You will know from your experience that it is easier when one change happens after the other, with time to adapt to each one before being hit by the next one. However, when multiple simultaneous changes happen, as is the case during primary-secondary school transitions, they can be more difficult to manage and adapt to, with psychosocial and emotional consequences for the child. Further, our and others' research have also found that it is the number and not severity of school concerns over primary-secondary school transitions that can predict peer problems, generalised anxiety, and depression (Jindal-Snape & Miller, 2008; Rice et al., 2011).

This might be worrying for you as a parent; however, it also provides opportunities to the school and you to intervene, by reducing the number of manageable changes taking place at the same time. As mentioned in Chapter 1, children could start visiting the secondary school whilst still in primary school for a year or so to use the gym or labs, there to become familiar with the layout of the school and some staff members. That will be one less thing for them to worry about when they are about to transfer to secondary school, especially given that children have reported that getting lost in the secondary school or having to get to know multiple teachers can lead to anxiety. If the way in which your child will be getting to and from secondary school will change, e.g., getting the bus and/or train/tram, walking, you could also practice this with your child in the summer break, so that your child feels confident and comfortable with this in September. This could also help to nurture feelings of excitement about starting secondary school during the summer break, and also reduce some of the worries children may be feeling, as one child discussed within our research: "at the start of the holidays I felt dead sad because none of my friends from my primary came here and then throughout the holidays got really excited and then the last bit I got really nervous" (Bagnall et al., 2020, p. 7).

For most children, feelings of stress and anxiety, dissipate within the first term of secondary school and positive feelings and experiences stay the same over time (Jindal-Snape & Cantali, 2019). However, that is not the same for all children, and if prolonged, and support is not provided, children who experience poor emotional wellbeing during this time, could be more at risk of poor academic attainment and social adjustment, in addition to developing mental health difficulties, which we have discussed in Chapter 2. Therefore, supporting children's emotional wellbeing, in the context of primary-secondary school transitions, is a significant public health issue, and will be discussed in the next section.

WHAT DOES EMOTIONAL WELLBEING MEAN IN THE CONTEXT OF PRIMARY-SECONDARY SCHOOL TRANSITIONS?

If we were to ask you as a parent "what are you most worried about in relation to your child starting secondary school" and "what is your biggest priority", you will likely say (and what we hear in our own research), is "my child's wellbeing, I want them to be happy, comfortable and settled at secondary school". However, from a research perspective, there has been a limited focus on children's emotional wellbeing, despite us knowing that children's emotional wellbeing is shown to predict their academic attainment (Vassilopoulos et al., 2018) and social adjustment (Coffey, 2013). Instead, most research focusses on the social and academic implications of primary-secondary school transitions.

Nonetheless, understanding how children's emotional wellbeing changes over time during primary-secondary school transitions, is important for us all, in order to understand when we should begin preparing children for primary-secondary school transitions, what this preparation should look like and how it should change over time. For example, from a school perspective should primary-secondary school transitions support work in class be continuous and span across the last two years of primary school and first year of secondary school (which we recommend, and draws on what we have discussed above), or simply just before and/or after children have "moved" to secondary school (inconsistent with our conceptualisation)?

In part this limitation may be shaped by differences in how researchers understand and subsequently measure children's emotional wellbeing in the context of this period, mirroring the conceptual landscape outlined in Chapters 1 and 2, regarding primary-secondary school transitions, and emotional wellbeing. For example, our recent review of the literature found that research studies are not fully capturing, in the child self-report scales they are using, the "context", in which children's thoughts, feelings, and behaviours are situated over primary-secondary school transitions. Instead, most studies are either measuring emotional wellbeing, or transitions experiences, or both. All three of these approaches are inadequate, as they are unable to holistically assess children's emotional wellbeing in the context of primary-secondary school transitions (Bagnall & Jindal-Snape, 2023; Bagnall et al., 2025a), which is important to understand as a parent and practitioner. For example, if children are not directly asked about their feelings towards the specific changes they are negotiating in the here-and-now over primary-secondary school transitions, e.g., making new friends, asking for help from new peers and teachers, getting lost; it is unclear why they might be struggling, and what we can do to support them.

CHILDREN'S UNDERSTANDING OF EMOTIONAL WELLBEING IN THE CONTEXT OF PRIMARY-SECONDARY SCHOOL TRANSITIONS

This contextual element in understanding children's emotions over primary-secondary school transitions is needed to understand how children respond over time to the social, academic, environmental and personal transitions changes they are negotiating, and how specific changes within each, such as changes in classwork, is impacting their emotional wellbeing both positively and negatively. This was shown in our pilot research, where Year 7 children (first year of secondary school in England) were asked to describe what (a) emotional wellbeing and (b) emotional wellbeing in the context of primary-secondary school transitions 'look like', if they thought they were the same, or different, and why, and what does this mean for adults. Emotional wellbeing in the context of primary-secondary school transitions was defined as "feelings which we've not had to understand before" and had an experiential and personal meaning to the children, representing new emotions that they must deal with as a response to new experiences that occur during this time. Without considering this context, emotional wellbeing as a general concept was discussed as not completely representing children's experiences and feelings during primary-secondary school transitions (Bagnall et al., 2024b).

TEACHER'S UNDERSTANDING OF EMOTIONAL WELLBEING IN THE CONTEXT OF PRIMARY-SECONDARY SCHOOL TRANSITIONS

In the same research we asked educational practitioners, the same questions, who also described emotional wellbeing in the context of primary-secondary school transitions as: "The emotional state of the individual during primary-secondary school transitions. This could be positive, negative or neutral" (Primary school teacher), and "The emotions associated with the experience of transitioning from primary to secondary school" (Secondary school teacher). Teachers went on to describe children's emotional abilities (which we will discuss in Chapter 5): "the ability to manage a range of situations and recognise, be in tune and manage those feelings that are associated with transition" (Primary school teacher), which mirrors what Year 6 (P6 in Scotland) and 7 (S1 in Scotland) children were saying with regard to the importance of "being able to adapt" or "showing resilience to changes" over primary-secondary school transitions.

To help teachers to identify what aspects of primary-secondary school transitions children might need more support with, we have designed and are now testing an easy-to-use scale that measures children's emotional wellbeing in the context of primary-secondary school transitions (Bagnall et al., 2024b, 2025b). The scale is called the *Primary–Secondary School Transitions Emotional Wellbeing Scale (#P-S WELLS)* and can be used in primary and secondary school classrooms to measure how children are feeling about primary-secondary school transitions generally, and also across specific social, academic, personal and environmental aspects of primary-secondary school transitions (which is theoretically underpinned by Jindal-Snape's (2023) MMT theory). Through examination of scores across specific primary-secondary school transitions domains (e.g., environmental, social, personal and academic changes associated with primary-secondary school transitions) and factors (e.g., problem-solving, self-concept, attitudes towards school), educational practitioners will be able to use *#P-S WELLS* to adjust their primary-secondary school transitions support in line with the needs of their classrooms, e.g., if their class scores particularly low on the social aspects of moving to secondary school, they can put in place activities that will directly help children to develop the social skills that will be useful during this time, whether that is how to make a friend, or ask for help from an older pupil, or teacher. To support teachers with this, we have developed a transitions curriculum, called **Talking about School Transitions 5–7** to use alongside the scale, which includes some "home-learning" activities for children to complete with yourselves as parents, which we will discuss later.

Through scoring of *#P-S WELLS*, teachers will also be able to identify specific children who are doing well over primary-secondary school transitions (indicated through high scores) and children who may need additional support. In the next chapter we will discuss, how parents can support their child with their primary-secondary school transitions, drawing on existing resources, underpinned by research evidence.

You can find further information here about *#P-S WELLS*: https://www.p-s-wells.org

HOW CAN PARENTS UNDERSTAND THEIR CHILD'S EMOTIONAL WELLBEING IN THE CONTEXT OF PRIMARY-SECONDARY SCHOOL TRANSITIONS?

You might be thinking, what does this mean to me and how can I understand my child's emotional wellbeing in the context of primary-secondary school transitions? And how can I identify that my child might be struggling with their emotional wellbeing in the context of primary-secondary school transitions? And how can I support their specific needs?

As mentioned in Chapter 2, spotting signs that your child might be struggling with specific aspects of primary-secondary school transitions (e.g., learning, social connections, finding their way around, being organised [to name a few]), might be slightly easier than spotting signs that your child might be struggling with their emotional wellbeing more generally, due to having a specific context to understand changes in their mood and behaviour. For example, to try and understand if your child is struggling with their emotional wellbeing in the context of primary-secondary school transitions, you might want to reflect on some of the considerations discussed in Chapter 2 in relation to the context of transitions to secondary school. For example, if your child is showing signs of being upset when coming home from school, or when going to school, it could be related to a specific subject or teacher your child has had that day, which they might be finding difficult. You could find out further information, by looking for any changes in your child's mood and behaviour when completing homework for this subject, and/or when talking about specific teachers, e.g., the "strict teachers".

If your child is showing signs of being upset after playing with friends online and/or in-person after school, it could be that your child is missing these social connections that they used to have at primary school, which they no longer have at secondary school. Try to remember the names of your child's friends, to help with this, and ask your child questions about their friends and what their interests are.

Similarly, if your child is showing signs of being upset following spending time on their own, it could be that this is the time when your child is reflecting on the changes ahead and might need more support from yourself, using some of the strategies that we will discuss below.

You know your child better than anyone, so if you are worried, try to think about the scale of your child's concerns, e.g., are they showing other, more general signs of poor emotional wellbeing discussed in Chapter 2, e.g., difficulties sleeping and changes in appetite, not interested in things that they usually like, withdrawing themselves from social situations and/or neglecting themselves. If your child is also showing these signs, your child might be struggling with their emotional wellbeing and mental health more broadly, beyond here-and-now primary-secondary school transitions-related school concerns, and might need some additional support from a mental health practitioner. To help in knowing the difference, we have provided a vignette, which discusses how Jasmine feels about primary-secondary school transitions (Vignette 3.1). When reading the vignette try to unpack whether Jasmine is experiencing difficulties with her emotional wellbeing generally or in the context of specific primary-secondary school transitions concerns, what aspects of primary-secondary school transitions these concerns relate to and what helped Jasmine overcome them.

VIGNETTE 3.1. JASMINE'S FEELINGS ABOUT PRIMARY-SECONDARY SCHOOL TRANSITIONS

Jasmine on the whole was looking forward to primary-secondary school transitions. She felt that she would be okay socially, with being quite a talkative person and enjoying making friends outside school in netball. She was also looking forward to joining her cousin Manu at secondary school, who was a couple of years above her. Knowing somebody at secondary school made

Jasmine feel comfortable that she would not be alone, as well as feeling safe about being around older children.

However, Jasmine did feel worried about the level of work in English and Maths at secondary school. She wanted to be a paramedic when she finished school and knew the importance of doing well academically from speaking to her dad at home, who is a doctor. Jasmine felt under pressure to meet his expectations, which made Jasmine feel stressed when thinking about the schoolwork and homework at secondary school. Her cousin, Manu didn't help at times too in constantly reminding Jasmine of the many changes she will have to adjust to a secondary school, which impacted on her ability to concentrate on her learning in class, with worrying if she would be able to handle them.

Once Jasmine had been in secondary school for two months, she felt like she had settled in. She felt confident asking for help if she thought she was lost when moving between lessons, and on the whole comfortable in her new surroundings. Despite worrying that she wasn't smart enough to do well in English and Maths in the first few weeks at secondary school, especially after what Manu had told her, she now felt that the English and Maths work was not as hard as she expected, and she had got used to the new ways of learning; she just had to persevere. Her teachers were also always on hand to ask for help if she struggled with a question, and her Dad was proud of the progress she was making.

In line with this discussion, Jasmine is showing signs of poor emotional wellbeing in the context of the academic components of primary-secondary school transitions, particularly relating to the change in the level of work in English and Maths between primary school and secondary school. Jasmine perceives pressure from her father to do well, and had begun to worry in primary school more generally about the number of changes she will have to adjust to in secondary school, which was impacting her ability to concentrate. This is in line with Attentional Control Theory in psychology, which is when our ability to concentrate is impacted by feelings of anxiety towards task-irrelevant thoughts (e.g., self-preoccupation; worry). This can cause cognitive interference, reducing the amount of attention we have to learn during times of stress. However, as shown in Jasmine's vignette, once we are emotionally settled, this is no longer a problem, as Jasmine found that the work wasn't as hard as she expected, as she got used to the new ways of learning, and began to worry less.

Jasmine also discusses resources and skills that were useful to manage her worries relating to the academic components of primary-secondary school transitions. In particular, Jasmine discusses "persevering" and "asking for help" which are internal and external resilience protective factors, which helped her to manage the demands of primary-secondary school transitions to maintain a stable affective state and flourish. These are similarly resources which you as parents can scaffold at home through activities and discussion to support your child's emotional wellbeing during this time, which will be discussed in the below sections.

HOW CAN A PARENT KNOW ABOUT THEIR CHILD'S EMOTIONAL WELLBEING DURING PRIMARY-SECONDARY SCHOOL TRANSITIONS AND HOW CAN THEY SUPPORT THEM?

Parents are consistently reported to be children's most significant source of emotional support over primary-secondary school transitions (Jindal-Snape & Cantali, 2019). This is unsurprising as parents know their children best, and because of this, children often feel the most comfortable in expressing how they are feeling to their parents, especially over the summer holidays before starting secondary school. As parents, this can be a daunting prospect, especially given that during this time you will also be negotiating your own significant transitions, alongside your child, which can be emotionally demanding.

Similarly, it is important that you look after yourself as a parent during this time, so you can best support your child. As parents, you might also be thinking how will I know about my child's emotional wellbeing during this time. Changes in emotional wellbeing in the context of primary-secondary school transitions can be difficult to spot, as there is a lot of uncertainty and unknowns for both children and you as parents, which can be both exciting and concerning. These feelings may relate to tangible changes (e.g., what will their secondary school routine look like, will the school day be different to primary school) and intangible feelings (e.g., how will saying goodbye to classmates and teachers feel, will there be feelings of loss).

Using Nicholson's (1984) work-role related model to our context, inspired by the initial application of it by Galton (2010), we can see that children negotiate four processes over primary-secondary school transitions which can impact their emotional wellbeing (see Figure 3.1):

- **Preparation:** children begin forming expectations, anticipation and anxiety in response to information about secondary school (e.g., induction days/weeks, open days, transitions interventions/lessons in class; which is shaped by how well equipped the child feels able to manage transitions changes and their emotions towards these changes.

- **Encounter:** children's initial experiences of primary-secondary school transitions. During this time, focus is placed on learning new routines and standards at secondary school and building connections with new peers and teachers.

- **Adjustment:** children are getting used to their new environment and expectations, and adapting their behaviour based on successful and unsuccessful experiences.

- **Stabilisation:** children are used to their new environment, have finetuned and expanded their skills and abilities to

The Transitions Cycle

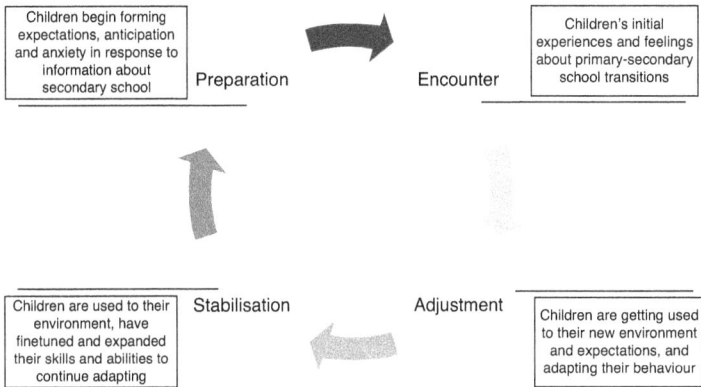

| Children begin forming expectations, anticipation and anxiety in response to information about secondary school | Preparation | | Encounter | Children's initial experiences and feelings about primary-secondary school transitions |

| Children are used to their environment, have finetuned and expanded their skills and abilities to continue adapting | Stabilisation | | Adjustment | Children are getting used to their new environment and expectations, and adapting their behaviour |

Nicholson, N. (1987). The transition cycle: a conceptual framework for the analysis of change and human resources management. *Research in Personnel and Human Resources Management, 5, 167-222.*

Figure 3.1 Based on Nicholson's (1987) Transitions Cycle, adapted to the context of primary-secondary school transitions.

continue adapting to ongoing transitions, including preparing for the second year of secondary school (where Nicholson's Transitions Cycle will begin again)

We argue that unlike Nicholson's model suggesting an end stage, as transitions are ongoing (Jindal-Snape, 2016), children will engage in continuous multiple cycles even over the course of secondary school, or in fact, in the same year of secondary school. They will also be engaging in continuous multiple cycles in other contexts, such as home or the community.

Psychological development at each phase is often an unconscious reaction to the demands of changing schools and the changing expectations of other people that comes with this, and we will use these processes to structure the below discussions.

However, first it is important to note that providing children routinely, with a safe space, where there is time for children to share their day with you, talk about their interests, how they are feeling (especially around critical periods such as school transitions) and ask questions freely is paramount throughout each of the four processes (e.g., at the dinner table). In fact, creating this safe space is definitely advice we would give to parents, as this will help to establish a supportive foundation for more focussed discussions relating to primary-secondary school transitions and something which we have found from our own research that Year 7 children find useful: "They told me about what high school was like for them which made me feel better" (Bagnall et al., 2022, p. 16; similar to Jindal-Snape & Cantali, 2019).

It is important that during these interactions, you are mindful of the importance of compassionate listening and "no wrong questions", which can help encourage openness, relationship building and trust, which is paramount during primary-secondary school transitions, as this can promote parents' continued involvement in their child's secondary school life, as they develop into adolescence. Through regular sensitive discussions within this space, as parents, you might be able to pick up on any changes in your child's behaviour (e.g., changes in body language, communication, openness, irritability, teariness) and outside this space (e.g., in sleeping or eating habits, social connections with yourself and their peers, changes in communication, hobbies), which may be indicative signs that your child could be struggling. Next, we will use the four processes to provide some advice on how you might know about your child's emotional wellbeing during primary-secondary school transitions and support them.

PREPARATION FOR SECONDARY SCHOOL (MONITORING CHANGES, AND SUPPORTING CHILDREN'S EMOTIONAL WELLBEING IN THE CONTEXT OF PRIMARY-SECONDARY SCHOOL TRANSITIONS IN PRIMARY SCHOOL)

It is common for children to begin thinking about secondary school several years prior to the actual move to the secondary school. According to children in our study when we asked them two years before transferring to secondary school, they had already started thinking about it in Year 5 (second last year of primary school in England) (Bagnall et al., 2024a). Therefore, as parents perhaps you can start looking out for signs of any impact on children's emotional wellbeing in the context of primary-secondary school transitions, as there might be changes over this period, and additional support needed. Be mindful, that they will be experiencing multiple transitions at all ages and stages; therefore, as parents there is no right or wrong time to be focussing on their emotional wellbeing.

However, how children feel about primary-secondary school transitions can be different from child to child, and over time for the same child, as the same research cited above, found clear individual differences in how children felt about primary-secondary school transitions in Year 5. This meant for some children, the usefulness of beginning transitions support in Year 5 was not realised until Year 6 when they understood their next chapter more through transitions awareness, exposure and knowledge: "Basically, at first, I thought it was unhelpful in Year 5 because I did not really have a clue about secondary school but then when we went to Year 6, yeah, it became more helpful" (Year 6 child), but for other children, the utility was immediate in alleviating concerns: "in Year 5, the transitions lessons were getting you prepared by practising things for when it comes" (Year 6 child);

> We started it in Year 5 because then we could use it into Year 6 and at our induction days but if we started it straightaway in Year 6, then we would not be as prepared for our induction days as we were.
>
> (Year 6 child) (Bagnall et al., 2024a, pp. 11–12)

Early concerns about primary-secondary school transitions can be especially prominent amongst children who feel that they lack control over the new and unknown changes they will negotiate: "It was a fresh start and at the same time like you don't have full control of it" (Year 7 pupil; Bagnall, 2021, p. 68, 69), lack transitions awareness about what is going to happen and/or how well their emotions and expectations have been managed in primary school:

> So, at first, I felt quite anxious about what was going to happen and then after participating in the transitions lessons I felt fine because at least I know what's going to happen and everyone's probably going to be in the same boat as me.
>
> (Year 6 pupil; Bagnall et al., 2024a, p. 12)

These concerns can lead to children feeling unprepared, worried about what is going to happen next, and reluctancy to want to become a secondary school pupil, as change is scary/unknown.

As parents it is important to look out for changes in your child's behaviour and belief system across Years 5 and 6, as this might signal that they are struggling with the above. Introducing discussion about primary-secondary school transitions early through a gradual and "non-threatening" progressive approach can be important in helping children to feel more comfortable about talking about primary-secondary school transitions.

A class teacher also supported an early start said:

> It was really good starting earlier, yeah. They were able to take it in more as well, than last minute lessons, you know, after SATS at the end of Year 6, they're more well prepared if they hear it beforehand.
>
> (Year 7 teacher; Bagnall et al., 2024a, p. 11)

However, for children with social, emotional and mental health (SEMH) difficulties, when to introduce discussion pertaining to primary-secondary school transitions can be more challenging. In our research, conducted in a primary school which specialised in supporting children with SEMH difficulties, we found balancing timing of when primary–secondary school transitions preparations should be initiated, and time to prepare children gradually for primary-secondary school transitions was a sensitive and an ongoing dilemma, subject to change each year to match cohorts' individual needs. However, what remained consistent was consideration of children's specific additional emotional needs and their perceived ability to cope when discussion about primary-secondary school transitions is introduced. For example, for some children introducing primary-secondary school transitions discussions too early, was shown to cause emotional difficulties: "it created a problem psychologically in the children here, because they don't want to leave and were quite anxious and worried going" (Year 6 Teacher; Bagnall et al., 2022, p. 5), and behavioural difficulties:

> A couple of years ago, we were asked to not come in [and do transition provision] so early as it left them with a few weeks of the boys being really unsettled, they were ready to move on, they were cutting their ties with the relationships they had got and it was making it quite hard for everybody.
>
> (Transition Support Teacher; Bagnall et al., 2021, p. 5)

In "Chapter 5: What is the purpose of primary and/or secondary led primary-secondary school transitions practices and are they effective?" we discuss some activities which can help you support your child's emotional wellbeing during primary-secondary school transitions taking a gradual, progressive and skills-based approach, informed by our Talking about School Transitions 5–7 intervention research. In "Chapter 6: What is the significance of primary-secondary school transitions for children and/or their peers who are living with additional support needs, including disability and health conditions" we discuss how activities and strategies can be adapted for children with additional support needs.

For some Year 5 and 6 children, emotional unsettlement about primary-secondary school transitions is shown to be visible through their behaviour, e.g., difficulties coping with daily routines, lacking motivation, and/or displays of acting-out behaviour, which one Year 6 class teacher described as "year six-itus": "so if we talk about the transition period, I call it year six-itus, they struggle towards the end knowing that they only have X number of weeks left" (Bagnall et al., 2021, p. 3). However, some children may internalise their distress. This might be because children find it difficult sharing their feelings through language, which can make identifying these feelings more difficult for parents. This was shown in the case study research discussed above conducted in a SEMH school, where children at times struggled to put into words how they were feeling: "I have bubby feelings inside my body about going to secondary school" (Year 6 pupil; Bagnall et al., 2021, p. 4), or preferred to generalise their fears during this time to universal feelings: "people sometimes feel scared" (Year 6 pupil; Bagnall et al., 2021, p. 4), or masked them, one child using an orange metaphor: "I have got a picture of oranges here to represent nervousness because oranges are actually hiding under their skin" (Year 6 pupil; Bagnall et al., 2021, p. 4).

If you anticipate that your child is struggling to voice their emotions, is masking, or generalising their feelings, it might be useful to use a prop or prompt to help your child to feel comfortable discussing what they are both excited and worried about. Within our own research, we have helped to scaffold identification and discussion about primary-secondary school transitions, using photovoice, vignettes and even fictional characters such as "Parker" the transitions dog. For example, the above research conducted in a SEMH primary school used unstructured and participant-led photo-elicitation focus groups, where each child was given a week to take ten photographs (using a disposable camera) of things that represented how they felt about moving to secondary school. In the focus groups, the children were given their photographs, and each took it in turns to discuss why they had taken each photograph and what it symbolised. This method was shown to be especially powerful in helping the children to feel heard and comfortable in sharing how they felt (including construction of unanticipated and meaningful responses) and gave the children a greater a sense of autonomy and ownership over their feelings by being able to present them through the medium of photographs. This an activity which you could do with your child, to encourage child-led discussions about primary-secondary school transitions. You could make a scrapbook page to visualise your dis-cussion, or even do the activity alongside your child to model the conversation, about your own transitions. In your discussion, try to balance feelings of loss towards leaving primary school with excite-ment and anticipation for new experiences your child will encoun-ter at secondary school, to maintain a balanced discourse, which will be discussed in more detail in Chapter 4. One helpful component of this activity is that it is child-centred, in that children select the topics that they would like to talk to their parents about. This is impor-tant to ensure that discussions are sensitive and guided by children's "window of tolerance".

Similarly, in another piece of our research (Demkowicz et al., 2023), we used a visually engaging storybook to ask children to imagine they were headteachers in a fictional school deciding how to help children and young people 'feel happy and okay' over prima-ry-secondary school transitions. This medium, adjusted to account for the age and stage of the participants, facilitated exploration of what might assist the fictional children to adjust to educational tran-sitions. This could be another activity which you could complete with your child, maybe if you are beginning school choice decision (where children and parents begin visiting prospective secondary schools and are then required to indicate their top three preferences in England) conversations, to help your child voice their thoughts about what they would like to see in a potential secondary school. You could encourage your child to create a list of things that are important for them to see in a secondary school, and categorise them based on "desirables" and "essentials". This will help your child understand how to go about making important decisions, and what they should be thinking about when making an adaptive choice, e.g., prioritising what is important to them. You could then bring a copy of this list with you to secondary school visit days, and ask your child to fill it in, to help them learn how to go about finding these things out, practise the skill of making informed decisions, and contextualise this learning outside the home. If one of the things on your child's list is not answered, you could encourage your child to ask a new secondary school teacher to answer their question, which will support your child's developing autonomy and competence and ability to ask for help. At home it could then be helpful to use this list(s) to guide discussions with your child about secondary school choice decisions (please note that in some nations of the UK, children automatically go to their cluster secondary school), and help them to feel empowered in having a voice in this decision.

If you are noticing that your child is quieter than usual, looks uncomfortable, and/or anxious when talking to your child about primary-secondary school transitions through the above activities, it is important that you reassure your child that you are there for them. This could be by spending quality time together doing things that they enjoy, to help them feel less alone and have a "safe haven" within this time together. If your child is lacking interest in doing things that they used to enjoy, encourage them to find activities that might help them, e.g., participating in sports activities/clubs, being creative, spending time with nature, listening to music. It is worth noting that children may also find change more difficult if they are already struggling with other things, such as mental health symptoms, including anxiety and low mood, or may be experiencing poor self-esteem and/or problems at school (as discussed in Chapter 2). If you are concerned about your child, it is important that you get help early, as poor emotional wellbeing can be predictive of poor mental health, and your GP and/or school could help.

Over primary-secondary school transitions, there can also be key trigger points, to look out for declines in their emotional wellbeing, such as around the time of secondary school choice decisions in England. Our research has shown that during this time, children can experience disruptions in their friendship groups, as children start forming closer friendships with classmates going to the same secondary school as them. This might be due to children feeling like what is happening to them is out of their control and could be a way of children taking back an element of control, in creating a support network, but this nonetheless can lead to a lot of peer unsettlement. As parent you might notice early signs of friendship changes, through differences in the peers that your child talks about at home or wants to spend time with at the weekend.

If you suspect that your child is concerned about social changes at secondary school, it might be useful to remind your child of times in their life where they have been successful at making new friends, and to talk about what was it about those social encounters, which made developing friendships successful (see Vignette 1.1). This will help to reassure your child that they do have the social skills to be able to manage friendship changes at secondary school. If you suspect that your child is still lacking confidence it might be helpful to provide some natural opportunities for your child to practice using social skills that could be helpful when making friends at secondary school, e.g., by encouraging your child to speak to "safe strangers" when outside the home with you, and/or encouraging your child to join an after-school club or activity. In "Chapter 6: How can parents support their child with their primary-secondary school transitions?" we discuss some activities which can help support children's confidence in making friends during primary-secondary school transitions, informed by our Talking about School Transitions 5–7 intervention research.

ENCOUNTER (MONITORING CHANGES AND SUPPORTING CHILDREN'S EMOTIONAL WELLBEING IN THE CONTEXT OF PRIMARY-SECONDARY SCHOOL TRANSITIONS IN THE FIRST TERM OF SECONDARY SCHOOL)

Above, we have discussed how to look out for changes in your child's emotional wellbeing at the "preparation stage", and how to support them. As your child moves into the "encounter stage", many of the same signs, e.g., changes in your child's behaviour, mood, routines, interests (to name a few) will be shown, and as a result similar support will be useful, especially open-communication about what is going well and less well during this time. In fact, as you can imagine from your own experience, and as seen from what the children and parents in our research told us (Jindal-Snape & Cantali, 2019), unlike relationships with classmates and teachers which are interrupted during the encounter stage of primary-secondary school transitions, parents can provide a crucial source of continuity and safety for children. This is especially important as other arenas of their life and sources of support might be in a state of flux (Jindal-Snape, 2023). Also, your strong and supportive relationships with your child can be more predictive of academic, social and emotional adjustment outcomes than factors within the school, especially when concerning the development of children's resilience, and when children are asked who helped them most to prepare for secondary school transitions; children almost always say their parents (Jindal-Snape et al., 2018). However, what is concerning from both a research and educational practice perspective is that although the significance of parent/carer support in helping children to adjust to primary-secondary school transitions is acknowledged, it is not harnessed in support interventions.

In part, this absence in provision may be subject to the fact that some children can be disadvantaged if parents cannot provide sufficient support during this time, whether that is subject to familial socio-economic status or language barriers (Jindal-Snape, 2023). Nonetheless, recognising how helpful you can be as parents in providing much needed emotional support for children over primary-secondary school transitions, we should be building on the strengths in families (Graham & Hill, 2003). As parents continuing to show an interest in your child's schooling and providing children with a safe space to talk and ask questions about how their day has been in secondary school is definitely advice we would give to parents. Emphasis needs to be on the importance of compassionate listening and "no wrong questions" nor judgement and can help children to work through any challenges they may have experienced during their day in a supportive environment, e.g., getting lost, forgetting a piece of equipment. Together you can develop strategies to overcome these difficulties next time, e.g., by brainstorming what routines could the child put in place the night before to check they have all of their equipment ready for their next day or whom the child could ask for help from if they were to get lost. This will encourage relationship building and trust, as children progress into their next chapter of life, as well as parents' continued involvement in their child's next chapter.

Feelings of loss, although common over primary-secondary school transitions, may be a sign that your child is showing poor emotional wellbeing in the context of primary-secondary school transitions. For example, as shown in our research, Year 7 children discussed leaving primary school as a significant personal loss in their lives: "like you were leaving part of like your family behind, and you were leaving part of like yourself behind" (Year 7 child; Bagnall et al., 2020, p. 8). In secondary school losing support, especially from primary school friendships, was a significant concern for children in mainstream schools in England: "like some friends you've been through like since Primary so you don't want to lose them and they're been through with you since Nursery, all the way here, so you don't really want to lose them" (Year 7 child; Bagnall et al., 2020, p. 8), and special schools: "I am worried that I might not see my friends because I have got some best friends here, and I might not see them at my new school" (Year 6 child; Bagnall et al., 2021, p. 5). However, this research also found that children perceived that this loss could not be understood fully by adults: "they didn't understand as much because like when they were younger it is different" (Year 7 child; Bagnall et al., 2020, p. 8), and therefore our advice for parents is to help your child by keeping discussions about saying goodbye to classmates and teachers at primary school open. You could also remind your child of the previous successful transitions they have experienced, such as starting primary school, or moving through primary school, birth or death of a family member, etc. It could even be useful, if you feel comfortable, to share your own feelings of loss in saying goodbye to your child's teachers, parents of their friends too, which can help in being relatable for your child.

Just be cautious to ensure that discussions are child-led, in line with their own "window-of-tolerance" to avoid transferring your own concerns onto your child.

It is also worth noting, that for yourself as a parent, primary-secondary school transitions will also bring feelings of personal loss that your child is growing up, and becoming more independent and taking on more responsibility. This can be difficult to manage as a parent, especially if this is your first time, which was mentioned by parents in our research: "I was very sad! I felt a little bereft at the thought of that period of his life ending and the thought of him becoming more independent and needing me less and less" (Year 7 Parent; Bagnall et al., 2020, p. 8); "I do not have older children, but I think this would have made a difference as it made a difference when my youngest started primary school, knowing what to expect and how the system works etc" (Year 7 Parent; Bagnall et al., 2020, p. 8).

However, as expressed in Hallinan and Hallinan's (1992) 'transfer paradox', which outlines how in order to gain a secondary school child's level of autonomy and maturity, Year 6 and 7 children must be willing to give up the support, familiarity and protection they are accustomed to at primary school; it is important that you as parents readjust in how you parent children to support and scaffold their developing maturation. For example, in the same research, parents expressed changes in their parenting role to facilitate their child's growing independence and prevent straining the child–parent relationship, through adjusting their boundaries to accommodate them growing up, and providing them with more responsibility, such as packing their own school bag, waking themselves up in the morning. This is important as children's feelings of autonomy and competence are consistently shown to predict adaptation over primary-secondary school transitions (Duchesne et al., 2017) and in "Chapter 5: What is the purpose of primary and/or secondary led primary-secondary school transitions practices and are they effective?" we discuss some activities which can help to support children's autonomy and competence leading up to primary-secondary school transitions.

Furthermore, similar to children, parents also must learn to negotiate new support relationships with other parents in secondary school, and reconfigure communication channels and relationships with the school, by transferring responsibility to your child, which can be difficult to manage (see Vignette 7.1), and as also outlined by one parent in our research: "I have to accept that he is now responsible for letting me know of any important information from school" (Year 7 Parent; Bagnall et al., 2020, p. 12). It is important that you look after yourself during this time, so that you can best support your child over primary-secondary school transitions, by recognising when you are finding things hard, by talking to family and friends about how you are feeling, and trying to find time to do something for yourself, that will help you feel better.

This is important as children can pick up on parents' concerns about primary-secondary school transitions, even when they are repressed. One teacher said: "the hardest situations I have found is where a parent is visibly nervous and agitated about the transition in front of their child, causing their nerves to be passed on" (Year 7 teacher; Bagnall et al., 2020, p. 9). A child also said that: "I don't think parents should stress that much, that gives kids more work" (Year 7 child; Bagnall et al., 2020, p. 9). As a result, it is important that, as a parent you speak to someone you trust about how you are feeling, so that they can support you in managing this period and provide opportunity to air your own concerns, as will be discussed in more detail in Chapter 7.

ADJUSTMENT (MONITORING CHANGES AND SUPPORTING CHILDREN'S EMOTIONAL WELLBEING IN THE CONTEXT OF PRIMARY-SECONDARY SCHOOL TRANSITIONS IN THE FIRST YEAR OF SECONDARY SCHOOL)

Above, we have discussed how to look out for changes in your child's emotional wellbeing at the "preparation stage", and the "encounter stage" but there are also signs to look out for at the "adjustment stage". For example, at secondary school children experience many simultaneous changes leading to multiple transitions which can be ongoing and emotionally demanding throughout their first year. Signs to look out for to indicate that your child may be continuing to struggle with their emotional wellbeing may be that your child is struggling to make new social connections with peers and teachers. It could be because they feel a lack of connectedness or belonging to their secondary school, which is not surprising, as during primary-secondary school transitions children negotiate significant formal environmental changes relating to the size and the structure of secondary school (which is often much larger than what they were accustomed to at primary school), but also informal changes relating to the school climate and ethos (where children are exposed to older and more mature pupils, as well as social interactions), which can be difficult to manage, and could lead to feelings that they may not belong in this environment yet.

This could lead to declines in children's interest in school, and if support is not provided could lead to poor academic progress. If you sense this might be the case, it would be useful to talk to your child about how they feel they are settling into school, and together think of some strategies which could help them navigate difficulties they are experiencing with formal and informal changes. For example, if your child is struggling with the size and structure of the school day, it might be helpful to support your child in packing their school bag the night before to ensure that they have everything they need and have completed all homework for the next day, and ensuring that they have their school timetable and map in their blazer in the morning each day. Furthermore, if concerns relate to being exposed to older and more mature pupils, it might be helpful to encourage your child to join a club outside of school where they are exposed to older children, e.g., Scouts or Girl Guiding, to help your child feel more comfortable being around and negotiating social interactions with older children.

In summary, if you are noticing signs that your child is struggling with their emotional wellbeing during primary-secondary school transitions, it is important that you continue communicating with your child in anyway that you can, even if it feels like you're not getting through to them. The focus should be on keeping the line of communication open and letting your child know that you are a safe person, who is there for them unconditionally.

STABILISATION (MONITORING CHANGES AND SUPPORTING CHILDREN'S EMOTIONAL WELLBEING IN THE CONTEXT OF PRIMARY-SECONDARY SCHOOL TRANSITIONS THROUGHOUT SECONDARY SCHOOL)

Progressing through the adaptation stage during the first year of secondary school leads to the stabilisation stage, where children are used to their environment, have finetuned and expanded their skills and abilities. For some children this may take longer, and some children may sadly not reach the stabilisation stage, especially if they are struggling with their emotional wellbeing and/or mental health, and have spent time in and out of secondary school for various reasons, e.g., exclusion and/or suspension, emotionally based school avoidance, family relocation. It is also worth noting that stabilisation is relative to each child's individual differences and journey.

It is important to note that we are continuing to adapt to ongoing transitions, such as preparing for the second year of secondary school. Before this next cycle begins, it is important to note that the stabilisation stage can be helpful in reflecting on the progress made in navigating the previous cycle. In the context of primary-secondary school transitions, your child's secondary school will do this through end of year reviews/school reports, parents evenings and award ceremonies. During this time, as a parent it could be helpful to take some time talking through with your child at the end of each academic year, the top three things that they are proud of and why, as well as three things that they would like to improve on next year and what skills would help with this, to demonstrate transitions as an educational continuation. Try to encourage your child to look at their first year of secondary school broadly, e.g., consider social connections that they have developed, a new environment they have navigated and maybe a new subject that they have learnt, which will help your child to see transitions as gradual and nonlinear, as it is likely that children will have navigated some of these changes sooner than others.

For children who have spent time in and out of secondary school for various reasons, e.g., exclusion and/or suspension, emotionally based school avoidance, family relocation, Nicholson's Transitions Cycle will begin again sooner. For such non-staged, age-graded educational transitions, greater support is needed, as children will not be making these transitions alongside their peers, unlike during primary-secondary school transitions which can provide a sense of "safety in numbers" and support. Furthermore, research has shown that unaddressed transitions difficulties can impact children's likelihood of future non-staged school transitions, e.g., exclusion to pupil referral units/permanent exclusion centres (DfE, May 2019). If your child is navigating non-staged educational transitions, see the below Encyclopaedia chapter on "Non-staged educational transitions" and if your child has additional support needs, also see Chapters 1 and 6.

- Symonds, J. E., Jindal-Snape, D., Bagnall, C., Hannah, E. F., and Barlow, W. (2023). School transitions in human and adolescent development. Elsevier.

TOP TIPS FOR CHILDREN FROM CHILDREN

1. Talk to your friends about your own feelings about primary-secondary school transitions. They probably feel the same about transitions as you do!
2. Talk about your feelings with an adult you trust. You could start this conversation by asking your parents about their experiences in secondary school.

3. Be confident and have a positive mind-set. To help with this, practise secondary school tasks, e.g., packing your bag, using new equipment that you will use at secondary school, using a map to navigate a new place.

TOP TIPS FOR PARENTS FROM PARENTS

1. Provide your child routinely, with a safe space, where there is time them children to share their day with you, talk about their interests, how they are feeling (especially around critical periods such as school transitions) and ask questions.
2. When talking to your child about how they are feeling remember that there are "no wrong questions or answers". This is important to encourage openness, relationship building and trust.
3. Over the primary-secondary school transitions period watch out for any changes in your child's behaviour and body language, which may indicate that your child could be struggling with primary-secondary school transitions.
4. If you are noticing signs that your child is struggling with their emotional wellbeing during primary-secondary school transitions, it is important that you continue communicating with your child in any way that you can, even if it feels like you're not getting through to them.
5. Remember that you are also navigating transitions alongside your child's primary-secondary school transitions; it is important to make sure that you are also accessing support that you need so that you can best support your child.

REFERENCES

Bagnall, C. L., Cookson, D., Stevenson, L., Jones, F., & Garnett, N. J. (2024a). Evaluation of a longitudinal transition support intervention to improve children's emotional well-being and adjustment over primary-secondary school transition. *Frontiers Educational Psychology*, 15, 1–17. https://doi.org/10.3389/fpsyg.2024.1252851

Bagnall, C. L., Fox, C. L., & Skipper, Y. (2021). What emotional-centred challenges do children attending special schools face over primary–secondary school transition? *Journal of Research in Special Educational Needs*, 21(2), 156–167. https://doi.org/10.1111/1471-3802.12507

Bagnall, C. L., & Jindal-Snape, D. (2023). Child self-report measures of primary-secondary transition experiences and emotional wellbeing: An international systematic literature review. *International Journal of Educational and Life Transitions*, 2(1), 1–31. https://doi.org/10.5334/ijelt.35

Bagnall, C. L., Jindal-Snape, D., Panayiotou, M., & Qualter, P. (2024b). Design and validation of the Primary-Secondary School Transitions Emotional Wellbeing Scale (P-S WELLS); the first instrument to assess children's emotional wellbeing in the context of primary-secondary school transitions. *International Journal of Educational and Life Transitions, 3*(1), 4. https://doi.org/10.5334/ijelt.79

Bagnall, C. L., Jindal-Snape, D., Panayiotou, M., Qualter, P., Banwell, E., & Mason, C. (2025a). Emotional wellbeing in the context of primary-secondary school transitions: A concept analysis. *Educational Psychology Review, 37*, 21. https://doi.org/10.1007/s10648-025-09990-6

Bagnall, C. L., Panayiotou, M., Jindal-Snape, D., Banwell, E., Mason, C., & Qualter, P. (2025b). *Design and Validation of the Primary-Secondary school Transitions Emotional Wellbeing Scale (P-S WELLS)*. Assessment.

Bagnall, C. L., Skipper, Y., & Fox, C. L. (2020). 'You're in this world now': Students', teachers', and parents' experiences of school transition and how they feel it can be improved. *British Journal of Educational Psychology*, 90(1), 206–226. https://doi.org/10.1111/bjep.12273

Bagnall, C. L., Skipper, Y., & Fox, C. L. (2022). Understanding children's, parents'/guardians', and teachers' experiences of primary-secondary school transition in the context of the Covid-19 lockdown: How can this inform transition provision now and in the future? *British Journal of Educational Psychology*, 92, 1011–1033. https://doi.org/10.1111/bjep.12485

Baumeister, R. F., Vohs, K. D., & Tice, D. M. (2007). The strength model of self-control. *Current Directions in Psychological Science*, 16(6), 351–355.

Coffey, A. (2013). Relationships: The key to successful transition from primary to secondary school? *Improving Schools*, 16(3), 261–271. https://doi.org/10.1177/1365480213505181

Demkowicz, O., Bagnall, C. L., Hennessey, A., Pert, K., Bray, L., Ashworth, E., & Mason, C. (2023). 'It's scary starting a new school': Children and young people's perspectives on wellbeing support during educational transitions. *British Journal of Educational Psychology*, 93, 1017–1033. https://doi.org/10.1111/bjep.12617

Department for Education (2023). *State of the nation: Children and young people's wellbeing*. Available from: https://www.gov.uk/government/collections/state-of-the-nation-reports-children-and-young-peoples-wellbeing

Duchesne, S., Ratelle, C. F., & Feng, B. (2017). Psychological need satisfaction and achievement goals: Exploring indirect effects of academic and social adaptation following the transition to secondary school. *The Journal of Early Adolescence*, 37(9), 1280–1308.

Galton, M. (2010). "Moving to secondary school: What do pupils in England say about the experience?" In D. Jindal-Snape (Ed.), *Educational Transitions* (pp. 121–138). Routledge.

Graham, C., & Hill, M. (2003). *Negotiating the Transition to Secondary School. SCRE Spotlight*. Scottish Council for Research in Education Centre, University of Glasgow, 61 Durbin Street, Edinburgh EH3 6NL, Scotland.

Hallinan, P., & Hallinan, P. (1992). Seven into eight will go: Transition from primary to secondary school. *The Educational and Developmental Psychologist*, 9(2), 30–38. https://doi.org/10.1017/S0816512200026663

Jindal-Snape, D. (2016). *A-Z of Transitions*. Palgrave.

Jindal-Snape, D., Davies, D., Scott, R., Robb, A., Murray, C., & Harkins, C. (2018). Impact of arts participation on children's achievement: A systematic literature review. *Thinking Skills and Creativity*, 29, 59–70. https://doi.org/10.1016/j.tsc.2018.06.003

Jindal-Snape, D. (2023). Multiple and multi-dimensional educational and life transitions: conceptualization, theorization and XII pillars of transitions. In R. J. Tierney, F. Rizvi, & K. Erkican (Eds.), *International Encyclopedia of Education* (4th ed., pp. 530–543). Elsevier. https://doi.org/10.1016/B978-0-12-818630-5.14060-6

Jindal-Snape, D., & Cantali, D. (2019). A four- stage longitudinal study exploring pupils' experiences, preparation and support systems during primary–secondary school transitions. *British Educational Research Journal*, 45(6), 1255–1278. https://doi.org/10.1002/berj.3561

Jindal-Snape, D., & Miller, D. J. (2008). A challenge of living? Understanding the psycho-social processes of the child during primary-secondary transition through resilience and self-esteem theories. *Educational Psychology Review*, 20(3), 217–236. https://doi.org/10.1007/s10648-008-9074-7

Ng-Knight, T., Shelton, K. H., Riglin, L., McManus, I. C., Frederickson, N., & Rice, F. (2016). A longitudinal study of self-control at the transition to secondary school: Considering the role of pubertal status and parenting. *Journal of Adolescence*, 50, 44–55. https://doi.org/10.1016/j.adolescence.2016.04.006

Nicholson, N. (1984). A theory of work role transitions. *Administrative Science Quarterly*, 29, 172–191.

Rice, F., Frederickson, N., & Seymour, J. (2011). Assessing pupil concerns about transition to secondary school. *British Journal of Educational Psychology*, 81(2), 244–263. https://doi.org/10.1348/000709910X519333

Symonds, J. E., Jindal-Snape, D., Bagnall, C., Hannah, E. F., & Barlow, W. (2023). School transitions in human and adolescent development. In *Reference Module in Neuroscience and Biobehavioral Psychology* (pp. 306–313). Elsevier. https://doi.org/10.1016/B978-0-323-96023-6.00001-4

Vassilopoulos, S. P., Diakogiorgi, K., Brouzos, A., Moberly, N. J., & Chasioti, M. (2018). A problem-oriented group approach to reduce children's fears and concerns about the secondary school transition. *Journal of Psychologists and Counsellors in Schools*, 28(1), 84–101.

White, J. (2020). *Supporting children's mental health and wellbeing at transition from primary to secondary school Evidence review*. NHS Health Scotland. https://www.healthscotland.scot/media/2964/supporting-childrens-mental-health-and-wellbeing-at-transition-from-primary-to-secondary-school.pdf

4

WHY ARE TRANSITIONS TALKED ABOUT AS BEING WORRYING AND NEGATIVE? WHAT CAN I DO TO CHANGE THAT?

INTRODUCTION

In this chapter, we will consider the primarily negative discourse around transitions in the environment which the child or parents inhabit. We will first examine the discourse at home, followed by that at school, in primary-secondary school transitions research literature and in the media. We will then discuss tips to disrupt this negative discourse.

There are times when we don't even know why we really love or dislike something. Our preferences are influenced by multiple hidden messages in the environment. A good example of this is someone like Derren Brown, a mentalist, who appears to have psychic powers but has revealed in his shows how he plants ideas/suggestions in people's mind by exposing them to words and images. In a similar way, we pick up cues from our normal, everyday environment. These might not be 'planted' there but nevertheless work in the same way. Several urban myths about secondary schools exist, such as the older children flushing a newcomer's head down the toilet.

DOI: 10.4324/9781032716145-4

These are compounded by what they hear from trusted adults, such as teachers, parents and people in the community. In our studies, children told us about the negative messages they picked from significant others. We are using the term *discourse* to discuss these verbal or nonverbal communication, as we want to focus on the persistent messages.

DISCOURSE AT HOME

VIGNETTE 4.1. THE UNFOUNDED HORROR STORIES

Jasmine was looking forward to starting secondary school. Her family suggested she speak with her cousin Manu about his experience of starting secondary school the previous year. Jasmine said that was a disaster! She got really confused about the lunch system as well as worrying that Maths and English were going to be really difficult after looking at the work he had done.

When we spoke with Jasmine after she had started secondary school, she said Manu had unnecessarily worried her. The lunch system was straightforward, and she found the work to be quite easy too. She said:

> You do get a little bit frightened about things before you are at the secondary school but when you're actually here it's better.

This experience of Jasmine about the discourse from family and friends is not isolated (Vignette 4.1). Several children have mentioned it over the years. It has been suggested that those who have already experienced these transitions, want to emphasise that it was not easy and recount the problems they encountered, to be able to then say that they were victorious and survived!

It is possible that children are also affected by the discourse at home which might or might not be due to the parents' own experiences of transitions to secondary school. For instance, in one study (Jindal-Snape & Foggie, 2008), a couple of parents reported that their experiences of secondary school meant that they still found it difficult to go to secondary school as a parent. Further, one parent who herself had moved secondary schools twice as a young person, reported that their child moved schools too.

> She just didn't seem to cope at all with moving up to the 'secondary school A'. Saying that, I was at the 'secondary school B' for first year and then I moved to the 'secondary school A' 'cos [because] we moved and I hated it as well so moved back to the 'secondary school B' for third year. So you can imagine what it's like now.
>
> (Parent 4, Jindal-Snape & Foggie, p. 14)

However, it is worth noting that this was a small-scale study and there was no robust evidence that parents' experiences did lead to their child having a similar experience. It is important to highlight that this could be a discourse related to the parent's own transitions in a very different context (e.g., workplace) for the child to be influenced by it. Therefore, it is important for parents to be mindful of the unconscious or conscious discourse that a child might be hearing at home. Families can play a pivotal role in changing this negative discourse by being more mindful of what messages the child might be getting and discussing them over time.

DISCOURSE IN THE SCHOOL

VIGNETTE 4.2. TEACHERS' DISCOURSE

According to Lisa, the 'preparation' from their primary school teacher for secondary school didn't help them at all, and

instead it worried them about how they will build good relationships with their teachers and how well they will be able to
do academically. According to Lisa, the primary school teacher
often said in class:

> You won't get away with this at secondary school you
> know. Teachers are stricter there. You also need to start
> working harder so I will start giving you more homework
> this term.

Lisa later noted that this was not their experience after they
had started secondary school.

As can be seen from Vignette 4.2, schools and teachers are
extremely influential in leading the discourse about primary-
secondary school transitions. Parents and children see them as the
experts and that what they say about transitions is likely to be true.

We searched for some examples of what schools have said about
primary-secondary school transitions on their website. As you can
see from Figure 4.1, worries and concerns seem to dominate the narrative. What is of particular concern is that the website in Figure 4.1
starts with 'Research indicates' without specifying which research
they are referring to but using that phrase to provide more credence
to their narrative. This also provides a picture of how research can

---

Key Stage 2 to Key Stage 3 Transition

Research indicates that the transition from primary to post-primary school is a significant and
stressful time for pupils and their parents. Pupils have to adjust to the changes involved in moving
from primary to post-primary school. Parents are naturally anxious about their child's ability to cope
with change. Most pupils adjust well to their new situation, but some struggle to cope. For some, the
transition can have a negative impact on their learning and social and emotional wellbeing.
Therefore, it is essential for primary and post-primary schools to work collaboratively to ensure that
all pupils benefit from a successful transition. Sharing information between primary and post-
primary schools is an important part of this process. A positive experience of transition creates
benefits for pupils such as increased confidence and improved learning outcomes. It also reduces
anxiety for pupils and parents.

Figure 4.1 Image of text on School A's website: Primarily negative discourse.

be used or misused, and also how researchers' discourse and poor-quality research can feed into everyday discourse.

DISCOURSE IN PRIMARY-SECONDARY SCHOOL TRANSITIONS RESEARCH

We saw earlier how research was used to frame the negative discourse on the school's website (Figure 4.1). This is of concern as after reviewing 96 primary-secondary school transitions papers, we found that 63% had a primarily negative discourse (Jindal-Snape et al., 2020). There were several methodological limitations in those studies, for example:

- data were collected just before and after the move to secondary school when everything is in a state of flux for the child, families and professionals
had a small number of participants
did not indicate the proportion of children who had a negative transition, implying by omission that everyone had

In terms of the latter, our own research found that, 42% children experienced a moderately positive transition to secondary school, 36% experienced a positive and 22% experienced a negative transition (Jindal-Snape et al., 2023, sample size 2559 children). Similarly, Waters et al. (2014) noted that of 2078 children in their study, 70% reported that primary to secondary school transitions were easy or very easy. This suggests that a large number of children will have positive or moderately positive transitions. Therefore, the discourse in research needs to be challenged. However, the number who did not find transitions to be easy or had negative experiences is still large, and we need to undertake further work to improve transitions for all.

Therefore, basing our discourse on research that might have limitations is dangerous. This needs to be challenged or at least not seen to be gospel.

DISCOURSE IN MEDIA: BOOKS AND FILMS

So what discourse are children exposed to in media? Has your child or you read Harry Potter? In the first book, Harry Potter is around the same age as a child starting secondary school. You see him escaping the grim life with his aunt and uncle and moveing to a fascinating magical world. He realises (as does the reader) that he has to learn a lot about things he has no experience of and finds them both exciting and worrying. This is perhaps relatable to the child reading the book. When Harry Potter arrives at Hogwarts school, he meets some really kind teachers and peers. However, he is also the target of animosity and is bullied by peers and one particular teacher. The latter makes his life difficult. Although the first novel finishes on a positive note, there are several negative incidents whose resolution the reader will not find out till, in the early days of its publication, the next book which came out a year later. This can create a negative discourse with some worries staying with the child.

There are several other books and movies that are aimed at children in the age group of 9 to 11 years which focus on change and a series of shocking incidents and fear of navigating a new environment. For the purposes of making things as dramatic as possible, the plots involve extremely negative instances so that later the 'hero' can be victorious. These can, however, leave deep marks on a child's psyche and affect their emotional wellbeing. As we are all situated in a social and media environment that emphasises and re-emphasises that primary-secondary school transitions are problematic, it is difficult to not be influenced by it. What we do not know is whether the books and films are simply a reflection of the (perceived) truth or do they actually drive the discourse around primary-secondary school transitions.

These negative discourses raise several questions. Are the researchers, professionals, senior students and families, providing a negative discourse which has become a self-fulfilling prophecy? Are they spreading the discourse that is negative based on the experiences of a minority of children rather than celebrating the positive aspects of primary-secondary school transitions that most children will experience at some point? Are significant others, such as parents and teachers, projecting their own experiences of moving to secondary school despite that being 20 plus years ago? Or more importantly, does the negative discourse exist despite positive transitions experiences? Is there a positive discourse that is hidden amongst the negative discourse? Is there a mismatch of discourse between different stakeholders? Where do positive and negative discourse arise from? And who holds the power to influence the discourse? It is important for us to reflect on these questions and perhaps to have this discussion with the child, parents and teachers.

Of course, we are not suggesting that some children will not have negative transitions experiences or if the numbers of those experiencing it is low it doesn't matter. Every child has the right to positive and successful transitions. However, when the discourse becomes negative with woolly estimation of numbers, then it has a negative impact on every child, families and professionals. It is important to be mindful that children might be more vulnerable and likely to experience negative transitions if their optimism level is not strong enough to counteract any high expectation of a negative transition, which the discourse in their environment may lead them to have. In Chapter 6, we will discuss in detail the transitions experiences of children living with additional support needs.

TOP TIPS FOR PARENTS

1. Be mindful of the language you use at home and look out for any hidden messages you might give unintentionally, even by using words such as 'the big school' or 'mind the big boys and girls'.
2. Don't take things at face value. Remember to question what you see or hear about primary-secondary school transitions.

3. Support your child in developing a questioning mind and problem-solving skills so they can question the discourse in their environment.
4. Create opportunities to discuss the discourse they are picking up from various sources. Take time to unpack any myths and why a negative discourse might be a story trope but not the same in real life.
5. Challenge the negative discourse whether at school or in the community, or in academic articles.

REFERENCES

Jindal-Snape, D., & Foggie, J. (2008). A holistic approach to primary - Secondary transitions. *Improving Schools*, 11(1), 5–18. https://doi.org/10.1177/1365480207086750

Jindal-Snape, D., Hannah, E. F. S., Cantali, D., Barlow, W., & MacGillivray, S. (2020). Systematic literature review of primary-secondary transitions: International research. *Review of Education*, 8(2), 526–566. https://doi.org/10.1002/rev3.3197

Jindal-Snape, D., Bradshaw, P., Gilbert, A., Smith, N., & Knudsen, L. (2023). Primary–secondary school transition experiences and factors associated with differences in these experiences: Analysis of the longitudinal Growing Up in Scotland dataset. *Review of Education*, 11(3), Article e3444. https://doi.org/10.1002/rev3.344

Waters, S. K., Lester, L., & Cross, D. (2014). Transition to secondary school: Expectation versus experience. *Australian Journal of Education*, 58(2), 153–166. https://doi.org/10.1177/0004944114523371

5

WHAT IS THE PURPOSE OF PRIMARY AND/OR SECONDARY SCHOOL-LED TRANSITIONS PRACTICES AND ARE THEY EFFECTIVE?

INTRODUCTION

This chapter will highlight the range of school transitions practices that are used across different countries, to support children and yourselves as parents. Throughout we have provided examples of activities and resources that you could use at home to support your child's primary-secondary school transitions and research on children's and parents' perspectives about what they found to be most effective.

WHEN SHOULD TRANSITIONS PLANNING AND PREPARATION START?

If like us, you see transitions as an ongoing process of adaptation, then primary-secondary school transitions planning and preparation should start as early as possible. However, despite a wide acknowledgment of the importance of providing early-onset transition support for children navigating primary-secondary school transitions

DOI: 10.4324/9781032716145-5

(Hanewald, 2013), transition support seems to be provided by schools immediately before and after the child moves to secondary school. In our research we found that even teachers who were from the same school, provided different time periods for when this planning and preparation started, ranging from two years prior to the move to a couple of months before the move to secondary school (Jindal-Snape & Cantali, 2019). However, are we focussing on the discrete activities that schools undertake to prepare the child for the 'move'? The days, they sometimes inaccurately, call 'Transition Days'? Is that the only preparation that is taking place? If that is the case, what was the point of going to nursery or primary school? As Alex said, don't they and other transitions experiences prepare children for primary-secondary school transitions (Vignette 1.1)? If not, how can we ensure that children's emotional wellbeing can be maintained during these transitions?

We believe that as far as the academic and social transitions are concerned the actual preparation happens naturally as the child goes to and through nursery and primary school. When we asked some children about the planning and preparation provided by schools for their transitions children were able to highlight these too (Jindal-Snape & Cantali, 201⬤pp. 1270–1271).

> I can work a lot better in subjects like maths because of the teachers that I got in p7 [final year of primary school in Scotland]. (Pupil)
>
> My primary teacher taught us skills that would help us in high school e.g. co-operation skills, preparing us for harder work and treating us like adults etc. (Pupil)

However, you will find that a lot of environmental transitions (physical and human) happen closer to starting secondary school, in most cases a few months into the final year of primary school. Saying that, as can be seen from Vignette 5.1, in some regions children start going to the new school to use their gym or science labs as far as two years prior to the move.

VIGNETTE 5.1. HEADTEACHER'S VIEW OF WHEN PLANNING AND PREPARATION FOR PRIMARY-SECONDARY SCHOOL TRANSITIONS STARTS

The headteacher of Lambeth Primary, Kiran, reflected on how and when children were prepared for their primary-secondary school transitions.

Kiran:

I suppose the question is when aren't we preparing children for their transitions to secondary school! The preparation starts even before they come to primary school. They are learning different skill sets, subjects, socialisation and everything else as they start and go through primary school. We gradually shift the difficulty level of their schoolwork, give them more responsibilities, provide opportunities to work in different small groups so they learn how to make friends, etc!

We also start sending them to our local secondary school, about two years before they are to move there. They use the secondary school's gym, music facilities, lab etc. Of course, as a bigger secondary school, their facilities and resources are exceptional. So it makes sense for our children to go there. But for me, it serves another very important function. They start going to secondary school without even thinking about the move in two years' time. And even if they think about it, there will be excitement about what they can do there. More importantly, they become familiar with the space and also some of the teachers and children they meet there or work with during a musical concert, for example.

If we view preparation from the perspective of the two children from our study and the Headteacher Kiran, if we can be certain that there is this ongoing preparation for different types of transitions, schools not undertaking concrete or identified preparation and planning till a few months before completing the final year of primary school can work. However, if schools aren't preparing children in an ongoing manner, then there is a problem… not only will children struggle with adapting to the new school, this is likely to have a detrimental impact on their emotional wellbeing.

What is your experience of this? Is your primary school preparing children in this way? More importantly, how consciously are schools preparing children in an ongoing manner and are all schools doing the same? Is this part of a plan or a hit and miss situation? That is the most important aspect that you as parents should be aware of and pro-actively start thinking yourselves, as well as asking the school about transition plans throughout your child's journey in primary school. Did you know that the schools in Wales have to share their transitions plans on their website? This is a legal requirement as a result of The Transition from Primary to Secondary School (Wales) Regulations 2022. As mentioned in Chapter 6, it is important that you are aware of your child's legal rights if they have an additional support need (see Richardson et al., 2017), as well as the school policy around transitions and enhanced transitions. Again, the law in Scotland mandates clear timescales and interprofessional/interagency meetings for this to happen (see Vignette 6.3).

In summary, schools should be preparing children for all transitions, including primary-secondary school transitions in an ongoing manner. It is important they plan and document these so that the purpose and outcomes are mapped over the years, and can be handed to whoever takes the baton from the headteacher or the class teacher. These plans should also include ways in which children and parents can be involved to support the transition plans. It is also advisable that schools stop using the term 'Transition Days' for a one or two day activity which doesn't even reflect a fraction of important activities that take place throughout the child's schooling. It inevitably gives the message, that children can be prepared for transitions in two days, worrying both parents and children rather than reassuring them that the child is 'prepared' for the move.

One point to bring to your attention is that, within transitions to primary school literature, a lot has been written about the child being ready for school or the school being ready for each child. Ideally all schools including secondary schools, should be taking an interactionist approach which promotes a mutual adaptation of the school and child, with willingness, openness, and readiness to adapt from everyone.

WHAT TRANSITIONS PRACTICES ARE UNDERTAKEN BY SCHOOLS FOR CHILDREN'S PRIMARY-SECONDARY SCHOOL TRANSITIONS?

It is important for parents (and teachers) to know what transitions practices are undertaken by primary and secondary schools to support children's transitions and why. They can then build on, at least some of them at home and/or consider what activities might be helpful to their child and recommend them to the school.

We reviewed good transition practices undertaken internationally (Jindal-Snape, 2010). Figure 5.1 summarises these practices, with further unpacking of their purpose and types of activities provided in the narrative. Please consider how parents can build on them.

We have summarised and grouped these practices below under the type of support that is intended to be provided and what form they might take.

(i) Familiarisation
Imagine planning for a holiday. What do you normally do? Do you just decide on a place and arrive there or do you do some research beforehand? These days with good access to places internationally, including street views and reviews by other tourists, we look at the places we want to visit and discuss them for some days. Why do we do that? We don't want to end up in

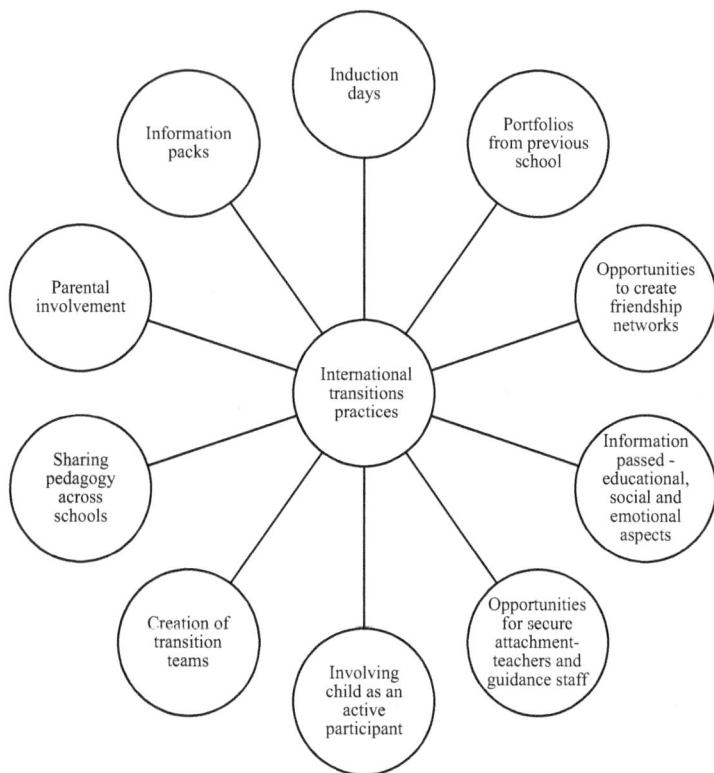

Figure 5.1 Examples of international primary-secondary school transitions practices.

a place and not know what to do once we are there. We consider how we are going to get to that city, but also how will we get from A to B once we are there. Even when we don't know the language spoken in that country, familiarising ourselves with the place, accommodation, transportation, food etc. give us a sense of confidence. We are not going into that situation blindly. Even if everything is not as we had imagined, we can deal with some of that small change or difference. The more planning we have undertaken beforehand, the more flexible we can be.

Now consider your child. What works for them? Are they better able to manage change when they have prepared for it?

Some children (and adults) have a functional need called, Need for Cognitive Closure. They work better when the situation is not ambiguous and they have planned for it. They find it difficult to function well when several surprises are thrown at them as we saw in the scenario with Sammy and the multiple balls.

Familiarisation with secondary school spaces, some staff and peers can make children feel confident as they will have some information beforehand rather than being bombarded with lots of new information and people when they start secondary school. It also gives them an opportunity to plan their route around the building as well as interact with some known faces, thereby reducing at least some uncertainty. With this in mind, schools usually undertake the following activities as well as organising some events.

a. Visits to the new school as early as possible, e.g., to use the swimming pool or other facilities
b. Staff and students visiting new school (virtual tours were started during COVID restrictions and are now available at anytime)
c. Induction days lasting at least a few days before and after the move
d. Information pack including photos of significant people and places that the child will encounter after the move
e. Starting a programme of activities which requires primary school children to visit a secondary school for a couple of years (see Vignette 5.1)

What else might be useful for your child? And, of course, you? Perhaps more visits, as would be the case if a child has additional support needs, but should be offered to every child? What could you do to make them more familiar with the spaces and people? One of the ways might be to try out the walk or bus to the secondary school over the summer holidays. Maybe consider what are the alternative routes or transport facilities so they have options (but without overwhelming them). If your child's school is not undertaking the activities mentioned above, or you know of other activities that might help your child, it is important for you to share them with the school, and as will be discussed later, teachers should be working in partnership with parents so this is a natural, ongoing process of sharing and learning. It might surprise you to hear that in our research we found that teachers were not receiving any training within their university programme and beyond to facilitate transitions (Jindal-Snape & Cantali, 2019). Most teachers reported that their learning came from discussions with other teachers. They might appreciate your constructive input rather than dismissing it.

(ii) Opportunities to create friendship networks

What matters to your child when they think about moving to secondary school? What matters to you about your child's transitions? Friendships! This is the most often cited aspect that excites and worries children and their parents.

We all want to make sure when we are in a new space, we have friends, especially ones we have known for some time. Your child will be no different. Also consider their developmental stage. They might come across as an island and not needing anyone! However, the reality is that when they are in a new space, they don't want to be seen to be on their own with no friends.

Let's look back to movies for their age group that show new children in a secondary school. They walk into the school lunch hall. All the tables are taken by groups of children and they are trying to work out which group they can or rather will be allowed to join. What will happen if no group allows them to join their table? What if they make fun of them? What have they learned from these movies? Either you have to be a good looking kid in designer clothes, coming to school in an expensive car (as the American movies depict them) to be able to instantly form a fan following and create a new network of friends… or that it is important to be part of an existing group from your primary school. To not appear alone or you might become the target of bullying. Of course, as we saw in the case of Alex (Vignette 1.1), there will be children who would like to move away from existing friendship networks from primary school so they can develop new friendships and a new identity. We also know that some children are relieved to move away from some peers who had bullied them in primary school. However, on the whole, research and practice evidence suggest that relationships with peers are very important to children. Losing friends and making new friends are also the most often cited worries they have (Jindal-Snape & Cantali, 2019; Jindal-Snape et al., 2020). Therefore, they should be provided opportunities to create friendship networks in primary and secondary schools. Schools do this in various ways:

a. Through co-curricular clubs and activities with other primary and secondary schools as well as in the community
b. Providing pupil buddies from the same and new schools, who are there to support them throughout the first year, and in some cases, for a longer period till the buddy leaves the school
c. School fair during the summer before the child moves to secondary school (opportunity for parents to meet other parents)
d. Residential trips where children from different primary school going to the same secondary school come together to undertake outdoor activities to get to know each other in a different environment. Some schools also undertake these trips a few weeks after children have started secondary school
e. Once children are in secondary school, teachers also provide opportunities for small group working that can help develop friendships (see Vignette 5.2 for an example of how it was done across primary and secondary schools; Jindal-Snape et al., 2011a).

VIGNETTE 5.2. THE GUITAR HERO PROJECT: WHAT WORKED?

In a local authority with a mix of large urban secondary schools and small rural schools, it was agreed that whilst children were in primary school, they would start working on a project that involved an off the shelf computer game called Guitar Hero. The Guitar Hero is a series of music video games in which players using games console and controllers play the roles of the lead singer, drummer, guitarist etc.

Ash and John told us about what happened as part of this project.

Ash said:

> When we were still in Appleby Primary, we started choosing song playlists and rehearsing some songs. The best thing was that our teacher didn't know how to set up the games console and she asked us for help. Anyway, we shared these playlists with all primary schools that were going to Abbeydale High.
>
> John: We then went to Abbeydale High where the gym hall was set up with several consoles which could be used by small groups. I was slightly anxious as I am not good at singing or playing the instruments. When we got there, we were told each band needed a whole team of different people, like marketing person, band manager, merchandise creator, financier etc. Now that excited me as I am great with making posters, badges… you know all the arty and creative stuff.
>
> Ash said: I decided to be the band's accountant as I love Maths. All day we had several teachers coming to see us. We were in groups with different schools. I knew no one! But we were told there will be a competition after we start secondary school… so we all started working as a team immediately. Everyone doing their best to make our band be the best one!
>
> John: Yes, same with our band. When we started secondary school we carried on working within our bands and teachers let us work on the project as part of their class. So in the computing class, we designed some badges and key-rings. In Maths class we were asked to calculate the costs, tickets prices etc.

> Ash: For me the best part was that we were learning different subjects as part of the same project, without even realising that we were studying! And also that when we met our guidance teacher, we were talking about the project, showing them what we had made… it was so much nicer to go in with something positive to get to know them… to break the ice sort of… before I went with any problems.
>
> John: The Battle of the Bands event was fun. Our families came to it and could see how much fun we were having. My dad said later it was so good to see me chatting away with my band members. I didn't know it but he must have been worried about me being able to make friends in the new school as I can be a bit shy at first.

You as parents can play a crucial role in this in your neighbourhood and wider community. We know from our research and experience that parents organise trips themselves, such as to the local activity centre, they invite their child's friends from primary school over for sleepovers etc.

We should also consider what message we are giving our children – friendships are important for us to function in a society based on that culture – however, can't a child be equally happy without their peers around them. Alex's statement that they wanted to move away from their existing friends had come as a surprise to us as researchers as we had till then assumed children wanted to stay friends with their very close friends from primary school. It was an eye opener and a reminder that during discussions about friendships, we need to listen carefully to every child's voice.

(iii) Secure attachments

Attachments that are healthy and secure are important for everyone. Your child will form these with family and friends at home, but they are equally important for them in school. They are useful for navigating multiple changes. Schools use different ways of doing it. As can be seen from Vignette 5.2, children built secure attachments with peers as they had a common purpose – that of winning the Battle of the Bands. Similarly, children who anticipate seeing their guidance teacher if they have a problem, in this case took their artefacts (e.g., posters, merchandise they had designed) to their guidance teacher in the secondary school. This enabled them to have the first one-to-one meeting with their guidance teacher which was positive, displayed their strengths and passion, with no perception of stigma attached.

Through one project that particular school cluster was able to do the following:

a. Creating portfolios or artefacts from previous school and/ or home take to secondary school
b. Building on existing and new secure attachments and support networks, such as with peers, parents and teachers
c. Providing opportunities for creation of non-stigmatised secure attachments with teachers, pupil support staff and guidance staff

(iv) Continuous open communication
Clear and ongoing communication is required between schools, children and families to know what the schools are doing to facilitate transitions, understand the child's needs and what they are excited or worried about. These continuous conversations happen within classrooms between teachers and children in the following ways:

a. Discussions about what to expect
b. Giving opportunities to children to talk about what they are looking forward to
c. Giving opportunities to children to talk about any concerns

Again, this communication has to start very early on. Also, it should be more than schools deciding what information and when to share with children and parents. Similarly, you as parents should take responsibility for communicating with the schools rather than waiting for them to provide information. Your communication with your child about what is exciting them and/or worrying them are important too.

A school-based intervention, which focusses on developing children's awareness of primary-secondary school transitions, understanding of the differences between primary and secondary school, and ultimately manages children's expectations and emotions, is Bagnall and Stevenson's *Talking about School Transitions 5–7 (TaST 5–7)* curriculum. *TaST 5–7* is a 17-week universal curriculum, which includes 4 lessons which are delivered monthly from April in Year 5, 9 lessons delivered monthly in Year 6 (apart from in May, due to National Assessments, and July, recognising end of year events), and 4 lessons delivered from September in Year 7. Each *TaST 5–7* lesson lasts approximately 40 minutes, and consists of individual, group and class-based drama activities, which aim to provide children with opportunities and a safe-space through a variety of individual and group written, spoken and drama based-activities to discuss their expectations, excitement and concerns about primary-secondary school transitions. Finally, recognising primary-secondary school transitions as an ongoing process, and the dynamic nature of emotional wellbeing in the context of primary-secondary school transitions, the curriculum takes a gradual and "non-threatening" progressive approach, e.g., by initially focussing on the development of skills, such as asking for help, and making decisions, that will be useful over primary-secondary school transitions, before directly discussing primary-secondary school transitions with children through a series of skills-based activities. Communication is a crucial component of the programme, right to its design which was co-produced drawing on the voices of children, educational practitioners and researchers; in addition to Jindal-Snape's (2016, 2023) *MMT* Theory, and the design and evaluation of Bagnall's (2020) *Talking about School Transition (TaST)* intervention, and experienced practitioner Liz Stevenson's *Transition 5–7* (2024) intervention, outlined in Figure 5.2.

We are currently trialling the *TaST 5–7* skills-based curriculum, alongside the design and validation of our *#P-S WELLS* scale development and validation research study (Bagnall et al., 2024b, 2025), and you can find out further information about the research here: https://www.p-s-wells.org/tast-5-7

The TaST 5–7 curriculum includes some home-learning activities, which you could complete with your child to support their primary-secondary school transitions. One activity which maps onto the theme of continuous open communication is the origami puzzler activity (see Figure 5.3). The origami puzzler activity encourages parent-child discussion about primary-secondary school transitions, through a structured child-led question activity. For the activity, children jot down eight questions they would like to ask their parents about primary-secondary school transition (e.g., what was your first day like?; did you get lost?; what were the school lunches like) in their puzzle. Using the puzzle template, the child then asks their parents these questions, to guide open communication and sensitive discussion around primary-secondary school transitions.

One helpful component of this activity is that it is child-led, in that children select the topics that they would like to talk to their parents about. This is important to ensure that discussions are sensitive and guided by children's window of tolerance. This is in line with what one Year 7 pupil said to us within our research:

> If they make too much of a fuss about it then it does proper worry you, it's like, like a soldier preparing for war like, if they give them a whole entire suit of armour it's then they can think, what are we going against.
>
> (Year 7 pupil; Bagnall et al., 2020, p. 13)

However, within this research, children also discussed the importance of honest exposure into what secondary school will be like to manage

HOW WAS TALKING ABOUT SCHOOL TRANSITION (TAST 5-7) INFORMED?

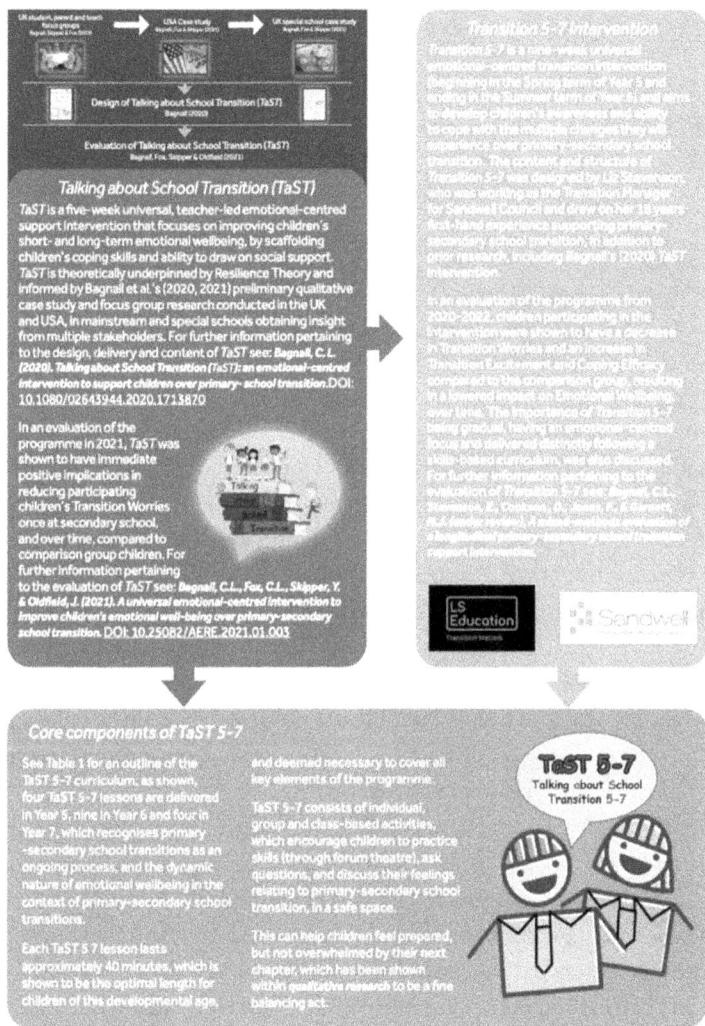

Figure 5.2 How Talking about School Transitions 5–7 (TaST 5–7) was informed drawing on Bagnall's (2020) Talking about School Transition (TaST) intervention, and Liz Stevenson's Transition 5–7 (2024) intervention (Copyright: Charlotte Bagnall).

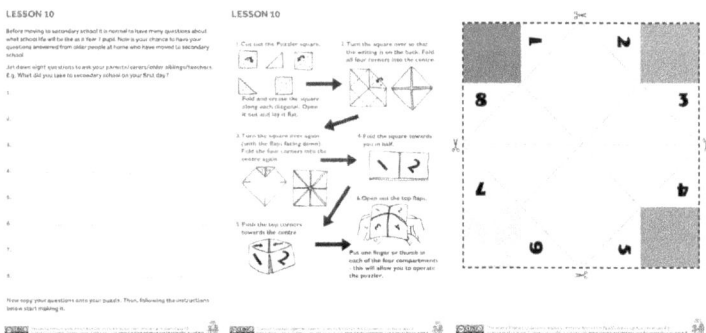

Figure 5.3 Talking about School Transitions 5–7 origami puzzler activity (Copyright: Charlotte Bagnall).

their expectations realistically; the main thing to remember is to stay within your child's "goldilocks zone" by providing a balance between exposure and consistency. In other words, children want a degree of insight into what secondary school will be like, e.g., for this activity while it is important that parents focus on the positives as opposed to the negatives, children will find it useful if parents provide honest exposure into what secondary school is like and don't avoid talking about potential problems, e.g., it is important to voice to your child that they might get lost, but focus should be on what to do if this happens so that they can prepare for this and manage their expectations. However, children also need, consistency, to avoid overwhelm and anxiety.

We created a board game on the request of parents who were not sure of what discussions to have with their children about moving to secondary school (Figure 5.4). Based on our research we added some words to the board game but kept them neutral without making any assumptions or judgments. We also included some abstract images on which children could project their own views of primary-secondary school transitions. A manual was produced to provide parents and teachers some advice on how to play the game at school or at home. You can print this or create your own board game to play with your child or children in your class. It can be played like any board game with counters and dice. The most important thing is to create a safe space for discussion.

Figure 5.4 Moving on: Board game to facilitate conversations about primary-secondary school transitions (copyright Divya Jindal-Snape, 2010).

(v) Information passed between schools:

Primary schools pass on information about the child which primarily focusses on educational aspects. According to primary schools, they also pass on information about existing friendship groups or where there might be tension between some children so that classes are formed accordingly in secondary school. This information is passed on to ensure that teachers in the school that the child is moving to, are aware of their strengths, support needs, friendship groups etc. Similarly, in the case of children with additional support needs, specific information has to be passed on to secondary schools, sometimes in a mandatory manner. Although all these are undertaken with best intentions, parents and children report that they are not aware of what information is passed between the two schools about the child (Jindal-Snape, 2018). It is important that there is transparency, and children and families are also asked to suggest which information they would like passed on or not. They might be able to suggest more relevant and meaningful information to be passed on which the professionals might have missed.

(vi) Creating a safe environment in which to rehearse transitions scenarios and strategies:

    a.   Rehearsing in a safe environment using creative approaches, such as creative drama, sketches, stories

    b.   Interventions to prepare children for transitions, such as *TaST* (Bagnall, 2020), (Jindal-Snape, 2012)

The importance of rehearsing strategies for adaptation to the secondary school in a safe environment cannot be understated. This can be done, for example, through creative drama by constructing a possible real-life scenario in which the 'actors' can depersonalise their actions and responses in the guise of 'playing the character'. Playing the guise of 'Robin' allows children to raise concerns in a more generic way as they are not 'my concern' but 'Robin's'. This creates a safe distance for children to experiment with solutions too. Ideally create such activities based on ideas that come from children during small group discussions. Based on the Forum Theatre approach (see Jindal-Snape et al., 2011b), Scenario 5.3 gives you guidance on how to create your own creative drama activities.

SCENARIO 5.3. USING CREATIVE DRAMA TO CONSTRUCT A REAL-LIFE SCENARIO: ACTIVITY FOR TEACHERS TO UNDERTAKE

It is the first day of secondary school. Robin is amongst the 120 children who have started today at St. John's High School. He is both excited and nervous about starting secondary school. His nervousness is due to feeling quite small all of a sudden after being used to being the tallest and oldest at primary school. When he is walking down the corridor two older boys, Terry and Joe, stop him. Terry says, 'hey Tiny Tim, do you want help with carrying that big school bag of yours?' Joe pipes in, 'we don't want you to look like the farmer's little donkey! Ha ha… but you do'. Robin doesn't know what to say or do. He's embarrassed and tries to escape as soon as he can. This becomes a regular event. What can Robin do to stop this from happening as it's really making him feel sick every morning before coming to school, he dreads walking down a corridor and it is affecting his emotional wellbeing?

Characters

- Robin (11 years old) is a positive and cheerful child. He gets on well with his teachers and other children. However, he is having problems with dealing with Terry and Joe.
- Terry (15 years old) enjoys teasing and name calling younger children. He thinks it is funny and will make him popular with other children, especially Joe.
- Joe (14 years old) follows what Terry does. He is under-confident but tries to hide it by sticking with Terry.

Creative drama activity

The teacher should ask the children in the primary school class or classroom assistant to volunteer to play the part of each character. The children who are in the audience seeing the scene mentioned above, are able to suggest what Robin can do and can also come and replace the individual (Robin/Terry/Joe or any other characters children want to be present in that scenario, such as a teacher or parent) and take over that character. (The facilitator asks the actors to freeze and then asks questions such as why do you think this is happening, what can be done, how do you think this person is feeling and so on.)

The ultimate purpose is to try to resolve the issue of name calling through audience participation and providing children with multiple strategies. Let children come up with strategies but if they are stuck, then the adults in the room can make some tentative suggestions. It is Terry and Joe's job to thwart any attempts to resolution so that a range of strategies can be explored, and children can see what works or doesn't work, and why.

For example, the children or adults can suggest the following:

- Robin should ignore the teasing and not engage with them.
- Robin should smile at them and thank them for their offer.
- Robin should avoid going on his own and walk with a group of friends.
- Robin should go and speak with his guidance teacher.
- Robin should ask his older sister who is three years above him at St. John's to intervene.
- Robin should ask his parents to come to school and speak with the headteacher about it.

Many other strategies might be suggested by the children. It is important to be mindful that this is about the children playing a character 'Robin' to ensure that they don't feel embarrassed or upset if their suggested resolution doesn't work. It is important, however, that there is a resolution so that the session finishes on a positive note.

Please make sure that check-in and check-out is built in to ensure everyone is comfortable and well.

Scenario 5.3 can be used to rehearse different aspects that are worrying children about starting secondary school, in a safe environment when children are still in primary school with people they know well. The safe environment and nonjudgemental stance through-out is extremely important, especially when resolutions suggested by children don't work. The active participation and creation of an armoury of strategies and responses they can use in similar real-life situations can make them feel more confident in similar situations at secondary school. With good communication from schools, you as parents could build on these strategies at home by carrying on the discussion and considering alternative approaches from different members of the family or neighbourhood friends.

The *TaST 5–7* curriculum discussed above, also uses Forum The-atre approach to encourage children to model and test-out different transitions scenarios, they may encounter at secondary school, includ-ing practical changes, such as using a school map; social changes, such as making new friends; academic changes such as packing a school bag; and emotional changes, including how to manage uncomfortable feelings and nervousness. These activities can help children to develop confidence and positive expectations towards primary-secondary school transitions, through strengthening their belief in their ability to cope, which has been shown within research to predict greater adjustment (Bagnall et al., 2021a). "Testing-out" learnt skills within the context of realistic scenarios in the safe space of primary school will also help children to form positive "habits" in secondary school. Parents can follow-up on these activities at home, by modelling tran-sitions scenarios, and "testing-out" transitions skills, e.g., by practicing scenarios where your child may need to ask for help from a teacher, or providing your child with opportunities to speak to other children they do not know, and make friends, e.g., through after-school clubs.

(vii) Active learning, participation and agency

  a. Opportunities to participate actively in their learning in preparation for transitions to different educational stages, across a range of transitions
  b. Opportunities and ethos suitable to developing agency in multiple contexts

We found that children found those strategies/activities to be most effective where there are opportunities for active learning, full and voluntary participation, and having autonomy and agency. The activities suggested here, such as the creative drama sessions, game play etc. can be successfully used for these purposes. These are also important for their emotional wellbeing, and to develop their resilience; in other words, children's ability to adapt to changing circumstances, while keeping mentally healthy.

We have discussed what we mean by resilience in Chapter 2, but we thought it would be helpful to contextualise this reading in this chapter, by discussing ways in which we can support children's resilience when thinking about primary-secondary school transitions especially.

Let's draw on Jenny and Lisa's Vignette 5.4 as an example.

VIGNETTE 5.4. WHEN SUCCESSFUL TRANSITIONS LOOK DIFFERENT

Jenny and Lisa both started secondary school at the same time and in the same local authority but different schools. When we met them after they had started secondary school, they were both finding the transitions difficult due to the bullying they were experiencing, and this was having an impact on their emotional wellbeing. They were being supported by their families, guidance staff, as well as in this case, their community link workers.

We met them three months later. Jenny had left their original secondary school and moved to a different secondary school. In comparison, Lisa had stayed in the same school.

At face-value, we would argue that Jenny has shown resilience, by remaining in their original secondary school, as she has persisted in adapting to that particular school, to try and overcome the bullying difficulties they are experiencing. If we continue reading the vignette, the pupils provide us with a bit more information about why they made the decisions they did.

VIGNETTE 5.5. WHEN SUCCESSFUL TRANSITIONS LOOK DIFFERENT

When the pupils were asked why they made the decisions they did, Lisa said:

> I have only been at the new school for six weeks but have already made two friends. The stress every night and every morning of having to go to my old school and how I might be bullied was making me hate school. I was feeling sick all the time. Now, although I am still a bit nervous at the new school, I am less scared. Yes, you could say that I am a bit happier even.

Jenny told us:

> I am still bullied from time to time and that makes me really upset… almost every day. But I am a fighter, you know. I told my family that I will not quit the school because of some nasty children! My guidance teacher has said I can sit in their classroom at lunchtime as that is when I am most bullied. I have got to know one child quite well as they go there too. I have also got to know a couple of teachers quite well. They are really nice.

In line with Resilience Theory, protective factors, internal and external to the individual, can modify their response to difficulties, and in essence their resilience. For example, protective internal factors can include a child's coping skills or their temperament, such as in the case of Jenny above, where she describes being "a fighter" and that she "will not quit the school because of some nasty children". In comparison Lisa describes feeling "a bit nervous about school", which could indicate that she might need some support with her **emotional wellbeing** and belief in her abilities to cope. External protective factors can also stem from the child's environment, such as their social support network, which can be shown in both vignettes, as Lisa and Jenny both discuss being supported by their families, guidance staff and their community link workers, as well as having friends. Jenny also discusses how their guidance teacher provided a safe space in the school environment to support them at lunchtime, and making friends is a reassurance to both pupils.

Some risk and protective factors, internal and external to the individual, are fixed and don't change over time, such as a child's biology, or are relatively stable over time, such as a child's temperament or their family structure. However, other risk and protective factors, internal and external to the individual, can be susceptible to change, such as a child's sense of belonging and their problem-solving skills, which can be shown in the vignette, as Lisa and Jenny's feeling of belonging at secondary school, is shown to be shaped by internal and external protective factors. This knowledge is helpful for interventions to help children, and Gilligan (2000) developed five key background concepts that underpin resilience, reflecting this:

1. Reducing the stockpile of problems (e.g., in Lisa's example, moving to a new school reduced the stress every night and morning).
2. Pathways and turning points in development (e.g., in both examples, Lisa and Jenny are moving from primary school to secondary school, which is a critical period in development)
3. A sense of having a secure base (e.g., both Lisa and Jenny discuss being supported by their families, and their community link workers, as well as having friends)
4. Develop self-esteem (an individual's subjective evaluation of their worth)
5. Develop self-efficacy (an individual's evaluation of their ability to perform specific actions, e.g., Jenny discusses how she "will not quit the school" demonstrating her belief in her ability to cope, what we call in psychology *coping efficacy*)

Drawing on these five key background concepts it is clear to see how protective and risk factors, external and internal to the child, are susceptible to change over primary-secondary school transitions. Thinking about *(1) reducing stockpile of problems*, it is common-place for children to navigate simultaneous, accumulating changes over primary-secondary school transitions, which in itself is a 'turning point' for children in line with *(2) Pathways and turning points in development*. Whilst the simultaneous changes children negotiate over primary-secondary school transitions cannot be removed, what you can do as parents is to help develop your child's perceptions of these changes, and ability to manage them, through practising some of the activities discussed above. Similarly, parents could sensitively and gradually, reposition school transitions as a progression, e.g., "a new chapter", as opposed to a loss. Parents could do this, by encouraging their child to reflect on a transition they have experienced in the past, which required navigating multiple changes across different aspects of their life (e.g., their relationships, their environment), such as moving house. Thinking about these transitions, parents could sensitively encourage their child to consider what was easy and difficult during this time, how they felt, what challenges they faced, and how they overcame these, to consider how this experience, and learning from this experience could help in how they feel about primary-secondary school transitions.

Research has shown that children who have been exposed to previous transition experiences find primary-secondary school transitions easier, often as they have developed coping skills and resilience from these experiences to use as templates in the future (Bagnall et al., 2021b), and reflection activities such as this, which are linked to children's real-life lived experiences, can help children to provide meaning to future events, and be especially helpful in the context of primary-secondary school transitions (Bagnall, 2020).

Negotiating multiple changes or 'stressors' within such a short period of time can have significant negative implications on children's ability to cope, especially if children do not have sufficient external and internal protective resources, outlined in (3), (4) and (5). Parents could model *(3) having a secure base*, through activities, such as the origami activity discussed above, but also by developing children's awareness of how accessing support from teachers, and classmates, might change at secondary school, how this might feel and what to do about this, so they feel able to continue accessing support. You could do this by practising scenarios where your child may need to ask for help from a teacher, or providing your child with opportunities to speak to other children they do not know, and make friends, e.g., through after-school clubs.

Finally, children with greater internal protective resources, such as *(4) self-esteem* and *(5) self-efficacy*, show greater adjustment over primary-secondary school transitions. It is important that as parents, we help to nurture these skills, through developing children's confidence in managing change, by practicing school transitions related skills, e.g., asking for help, using a map, making new friends, as shown though the activities above which model and test-out different transition scenarios, including practical changes, such as using a school map; social changes, such as making new friends; academic changes such as packing a school bag; and emotional changes, including how to manage uncomfortable feelings and nervousness. These activities can help children to develop confidence and positive expectations towards primary-secondary school transitions, through strengthening their belief in their ability to cope, which has been shown within research to predict greater adjustment (Bagnall et al., 2021a).

It is also worth noting that exposure to risk is not a bad thing. Exposure, as opposed to avoidance to low-level risk or challenge can be positive and an essential part of your child's development. What is needed nonetheless though is sensitivity to your child's window of tolerance.

(viii) Collaborative partnership between schools and parents

    a.   Sharing pedagogy across schools
    b.   Parental participation

There is ample evidence that collaborative partnerships are key to facilitating seamless and positive transitions. These include teachers from primary and secondary schools working in each others' classes so that they can learn about the pedagogical approaches teachers use at different educational stages. Similarly, some schools try to have effective and ongoing partnerships with parents so that they can get better insights about each individual child's strengths and support needs. What is your experience of this so far? In some cases, there are strong parents' councils that are involved by schools in transitions planning and preparation. However, this is not done as often as one would hope to see.

(ix) Creation of transition teams

In some regions, transitions teachers have been appointed who have the overall responsibility for transitions planning and preparation. These transitions teachers are also provided space to undertake relevant training as well as training other teachers. However, it seems that overtime these posts have been dissolved by cash poor local authorities despite some evidence of their effectiveness. Although their visibility in that role is helpful, for families and other teachers, there is a concern that everyone then sees them as being responsible for everything to do with transitions. Transitions need to be everyone's business and can't be left to a named few people. More research is required to determine the effectiveness of transitions teachers.

The transitions practice can also be considered as five bridges of transfer (Galton & McLellan, 2018). Galton and colleagues summarised it as:

(i) Administrative: to ease the transfer process through meetings of head teachers and transfer of information
(ii) Social/ User Friendly: to ease children's anxieties through familiarisation through open days and induction events
(iii) Curriculum: considering curricular continuity and progression, some schools used bridging units, same worksheets across the final year of primary and first year of secondary school
(iv) Pedagogy: to enhance pedagogical continuity, with teachers taking classes in visiting schools and through observation

(v) Managing learning: to develop children as professional learners with some relevant activities through programmes such as 'Learning to learn'

COVID-19, interestingly, led to better transitions practices from the perspective of some teachers. Edge et al. (2023, p. 24) study found that teachers in England and Wales started thinking outside the box (See Chapter 7):

> …it's made me appreciate the importance of transition more, and think more about what the children need from it rather than it being, a task that you have to do. It's much more about, now what do the children and the families need to get from it?
> (Transition Lead, School G, England, FSM (Free School Meal) 11–20%)

In this study, parents also reported that the virtual sessions were effective:

> The parent feedback who have emailed in said, thanks ever so much a great evening it was fabulous to be able to ask questions and not have to say it but just put it into the comment boxes, and I had someone on the chat box answering the comments as they were coming in. (Transition Lead, School I, Wales, FSM 0–10%).
> (Edge et al., 2023, p. 24)

WHAT TRANSITIONS PRACTICES ARE UNDERTAKEN BY SCHOOLS TO SUPPORT PARENTS' TRANSITIONS AND TO SUPPORT THEIR CHILD'S PRIMARY-SECONDARY SCHOOL TRANSITIONS?

It is important to consider transitions practices from the parents' perspective and what support should be provided to them for their own transitions and to support their children with their transitions. Unfortunately, there is very little that is done for parents' transitions even when triggered by their child's primary-secondary school transitions; mainly due to the absence of understanding of parental transitions and the multi-dimensional nature of transitions. This is problematic as you will know yourself that you can't support your children effectively if you are in the middle of managing your own transitions. This is also confounded by the fact that not all parents view their child's transitions to be triggering transitions for them (Jindal-Snape & Cantali, 2019). As can be seen by the quotations below (Jindal-Snape & Cantali, unpublished data), when asked about what schools could have done for their transitions, parents only focussed on accurate and timely information from schools about arrangements for their child:

> There was a bit of miscommunication from the school in terms of dates/times for transition meetings, which was unhelpful. Other than that, I feel that the school have done quite well in preparing parents. (Parent of secondary school pupil)

> I would have liked to have been given more information about the transport situation sooner. I still feel like I am not 100% clear on the arrangements and I will have to find out more information myself. I would also really liked to have had information about extra-curricular activities sent out so that I could chat to my son about what he might like to try before he starts school. Otherwise, the information provided has been helpful. (Parent of secondary school pupil)

WHAT DO CHILDREN SAY ABOUT THE EFFECTIVENESS OF SCHOOLS' TRANSITIONS PRACTICES?

In our research, we found that children's views about the effectiveness of school transitions practices seem to change over time (Jindal-Snape & Cantali, 2019). Perhaps this is not surprising as their needs change over time as well as what was useful when preparing to leave primary school might not be in secondary school. However, there was consensus about some beneficial aspects of the practices, namely, early start of the familiarisation with the new environment, both human and physical; residential and class trips that gave them more independence and responsibility; induction visits to the secondary school; visit of the secondary school headteacher, guidance teacher and older children to their school who could answer their queries; preparation for higher level academic work required in the secondary school; and classroom discussions with primary school teachers about what to expect in secondary school.

TOP TIPS FOR PRIMARY AND SECONDARY SCHOOL TEACHERS FROM CHILDREN AND PARENTS

1. Transitions practices should explicitly focus on enhancing children, parents and teachers' emotional wellbeing. Consider the importance of collective and multiple and multi-dimensional emotional wellbeing.
2. Start the familiarisation with the potential destination secondary school as early as possible. This should be done for both children and parents. Children with additional support needs might require an even longer time frame for familiarisation.
3. Provide opportunities for children to have discussions about what they are excited about or worried about before they start secondary school and follow these up in secondary school to understand any emerging excitement/worries.
4. Provide opportunities for children to learn to form friendships with different children, e.g., through small group work.
5. Ensure that children feel they have a choice over and voice in decisions made about them. The same applies to their parents.
6. Use resources available to support with children's transitions but also create your own that are specific to the children you are working with.

7. Ask children and parents what transitions practices would be most useful for them as well as what worked well for them once they were in secondary school. There should be a feedback loop back to primary schools facilitated by secondary schools.

8. Familiarise yourself with the relevant legislation and school policies to ensure that you understand your responsibilities in supporting different children and families.

9. Increase the frequency and duration of secondary school staff and children's visit to linked primary school.

10. Provide positive opportunities for primary school children to visit secondary school, such as annual games and concerts.

11. Understand children and families multiple and multi-dimensional transitions and consider their holistic support needs.
    Understand your own multiple and multi-dimensional transitions and consider your own support needs.

12. Identify your training needs related to supporting children and families with primary-secondary school transitions and access such training.

REFERENCES

Bagnall, C. L. (2020). Talking about School Transition (TaST): An emotional centred intervention to support children over primary-secondary school transition. *Pastoral Care in Education*, 1–22. https://doi.org/10.1080/02643944.2020.1713870

Bagnall, C. L., Fox, C. L., Skipper, Y., & Oldfield, J. (2021a). Evaluating a universal emotional-centred intervention to improve children's emotional well-being over primary-secondary school transition. *Advances in Educational Research and Evaluation*, 2, 113–126. https://doi.org/10.25082/AERE.2021.01.003

Bagnall, C. L., Cookson, D., Stevenson, L., Jones, F., & Garnett, N. J. (2024a). Evaluation of a longitudinal transition support intervention to improve children's emotional well-being and adjustment over primary-secondary school transition. *Frontiers Educational Psychology*, 15, 1–17. https://doi.org/10.3389/fpsyg.2024.1252851

Bagnall, C. L., Fox, C. L., & Skipper, Y. (2021b). When is the 'optimal' time for school transition? An insight into provision in the US. Pastoral Care in Education, 39(4), 348-376. https://doi.org/10.1080/02643944.2020.1855669

Bagnall, C. L., Jindal-Snape, D., Panayiotou, M., & Qualter, P. (2024b). Design and validation of the Primary-Secondary School Transitions Emotional Wellbeing Scale (P-S WELLS); the first instrument to assess children's emotional wellbeing in the context of primary-secondary school transitions. *International Journal of Educational and Life Transitions,* 3(1), 4. https://doi.org/10.5334/ijelt.79

Bagnall, C. L., Panayiotou, M., Jindal-Snape, D., Banwell, E., Mason, C., & Qualter, P. (2025). *Design and Validation of the Primary-Secondary school Transitions Emotional Wellbeing Scale (P-S WELLS). Assessment,* 1–16. DOI: 10.1177/10731911251332241

Bagnall, C. L., Skipper, Y., & Fox, C. L. (2020). 'You're in this world now': Students', teachers', and parents' experiences of school transition and how they feel it can be improved. *British Journal of Educational Psychology*, 90(1), 206–226. https://doi.org/10.1111/bjep.12273

Edge, D., Redwood, S., Jindal-Snape, D., & Crawley, E. (2023). Impact of COVID-19 pandemic on secondary school teaching staff and primary to secondary transitions. *Psychology in the Schools*, 61(1), 17–28. https://doi.org/10.1002/pits.23017

Galton, M., & McLellan, R. (2018). A transition Odyssey: Pupils' experiences of transfer to secondary school across five decades. *Research Papers in Education*, 33(2), 255–277. https://doi.org/10.1080/02671522.2017.1302496

Gilligan, R. (2000). Adversity, resilience and young people: The protective value of positive school and spare time experiences. *Children & Society*, 14(1), 37–47.

Hanewald (2013). Transition between primary and secondary school: Why it is important and how it can be supported. *Australian Journal of Teacher Education*, 38(1), 62–74. https://doi.org/10.14221/ajte.2013v38n1.7

Jindal-Snape, D. (2010, February). Five years left until 2015: What should be our priority?. In *Publisher is Japan Education Forum VII* (p. 58).

Jindal-Snape, D., Baird, L., & Miller, K. (2011a). A longitudinal study to investigate the effectiveness of the Guitar Hero project in supporting transition from P7-S1. Dundee: Report for Learning and Teaching Scotland.

Jindal-Snape, D. (2012). Portraying children's voices through creative approaches to enhance their transition experience and improve the transition practice. *Learning Landscapes*, 6(1), 223–240. https://www.learninglandscapes.ca/

Jindal-Snape, D. (2016). *The A–Z of Transitions*. Palgrave Macmillan.

Jindal-Snape, D. (2018). Transitions from early years to primary and primary to secondary schools in Scotland. In T. Bryce, W. Humes, D. Gillies, & A. Kennedy (Eds.), *Scottish Education* (5th ed.). Edinburgh University Press.

Jindal-Snape, D., Hannah, E. F., Cantali, D., Barlow, W., & MacGillivray, S. (2020). Systematic literature review of primary-secondary transitions: International research. Review of Education, 8(2), 526-566. https://doi.org/10.1002/rev3.3197

Jindal-Snape, D. (2022). Conceptualising and theorising primary-secondary transitions. In S. Capel, M. Leask, S. Younie , E. Hidson , & J. Lawrence (Eds.), Learning to teach in the secondary school : A companion to school experience (9 ed., pp. 190-204). Routledge. https://doi.org/10.4324/9781003201267-16

Jindal-Snape, D. (2023). Multiple and multi-dimensional educational and life transitions: conceptualization, theorization and XII pillars of transitions. In R. J. Tierney, F. Rizvi, & K. Erkican (Eds.), *International Encyclopedia of Education* (4th ed., pp. 530–543). Elsevier. https://doi.org/10.1016/B978-0-12-818630-5.14060-6

Jindal-Snape, D., & Cantali, D. (2019). A four-stage longitudinal study exploring pupils' experiences, preparation and support systems during primary–secondary school transitions. *British Educational Research Journal*, 45(6), 1255–1278. https://doi.org/10.1002/berj.3561

Jindal-Snape, D., Vettraino, E., Lowson, A., & McDuff, W. (2011b). Using creative drama to facilitate primary–secondary transition. *Education 3–13*, 39(4), 383–394. https://doi.org/10.1080/03004271003727531

Richardson, T. D., Jindal-Snape, D., & Hannah, E. F. S. (2017). Impact of Legislation on Post-School Transition Practice for young people with additional support needs in Scotland. *British Journal of Special Education*, 44(3), 239–256. https://doi.org/10.1111/1467-8578.12178

The Transition from Primary to Secondary School (Wales) Regulations 2022 (Accessed on 6.3.25 Transition from primary to secondary school guidance - Hwb).

6

WHAT IS THE SIGNIFICANCE OF PRIMARY-SECONDARY SCHOOL TRANSITIONS FOR A CHILD AND/OR THEIR PEERS WHO ARE LIVING WITH ADDITIONAL SUPPORT NEEDS, INCLUDING DISABILITY AND HEALTH CONDITIONS?

INTRODUCTION

In this chapter, we will focus on the impact of additional support needs on children's transitions experiences and why it is important for parents and teachers to be familiar with the legislation the schools have to abide by. We also highlight how schools have sometimes failed children living with additional support needs and their families. Following this, we discuss voice, child-centred planning and child-parent-school partnership. It is important to note that although these have been discussed in the context of additional support needs, these are relevant to every child and family, if we want to ensure inclusive and meaningful transitions practices.

DOI: 10.4324/9781032716145-6

Finally, we have discussed two examples of how children's voice can be heard and they can be the centre of any decision-making. We have also used vignettes based on real cases to exemplify the various aspects.

WHAT IS THE IMPACT OF ADDITIONAL SUPPORT NEEDS ON CHILDREN'S TRANSITIONS EXPERIENCES?

VIGNETTE 6.1. TOM'S TRANSITIONS EXPERIENCES

Tom has muscular dystrophy. He found that his experience in primary and secondary school was very different. He said:

> When I was in primary school, I was treated the same. I joined my class on trips. I was starting to have some falls by the end of primary so I started using a wheelchair. I was still treated in the same way as before.
>
> When I was starting the second year in secondary school, the headteacher put me in a lower class because my year group's room was upstairs and there was no lift. I lost the friends I had made in the first year. I also felt that they thought I wasn't clever enough, you know… that really upset me and I found it difficult to deal with.

Tom went on to explain the impact of the environmental transitions on him which had nothing to do with his disability and more to do with the systems not being geared to adapt and the attitude of one individual at secondary school. This had substantial impact on his mental health and emotional wellbeing.

It is important to note that in subsequent conversations when he was older and leaving secondary school, he was not given the same choices as his peers. Tom said:

> All my classmates went to uni. I wanted to go to uni but I wasn't even given that option! It was like I was being told again and again and again that I wasn't clever enough!
> When I was around 21 years old, I thought enough is enough and enrolled on to the Open University programme. I not only completed an undergraduate but also a postgraduate degree. Why did I have to waste my time? Why couldn't the headteacher look beyond my wheelchair? It was emotionally such a terrible time for me! And now, I am just furious! Happy but also furious.

Depending on the country you are in, the child might already have a planned move to a secondary school (i.e., a default move from one primary to secondary, including moving from mainstream primary to mainstream secondary, mainstream primary to special school or special school to special school).

In this book, we have used the term additional support needs. Children can be living with additional support needs for a range of reasons, including disabilities, chronic health conditions, death of a significant other, English as an additional language, children in care, etc. Research suggests that children living with additional support needs might be more vulnerable to negative transitions experiences, due to anxiety and stress that children and families can experience (Hannah & Topping, 2012), problems with dealing with change (Peters & Brooks, 2016), the noise and hustle in their larger secondary school making autistic children feel unsafe (Dillon & Underwood, 2012), and acoustics in some spaces being uncomfortable (Lightfoot & Bond, 2013).

However, as most of the studies had very few participants (e.g., five children) and they did not, in the main, look at any differences between children who have an identified additional support need and their peers who don't, it is difficult to generalise the findings of these studies. However, in a larger study, we did find that children with additional support needs were less likely to have positive transitions and more likely to have negative transitions than their peers who did not have any identified additional support needs (Jindal-Snape et al., 2023). We found that of the children who had additional support needs either in primary and/or secondary school, 26% experienced positive and 32% negative transitions. However, of the children with no identified additional support needs, 39% had a positive and 19% a negative transition to secondary school.

On a more positive note, we should note that 26% of children with additional support needs in this study did have positive transitions experiences. Similarly, although in a study with a very small sample, autistic children reported having positive transitions experiences due to the impact of clear structure and routine in secondary school which they thought was missing in primary school (Neal & Frederickson, 2016). As we saw in Tom's case, children's transitions were not only impacted by the complexity or severity of their additional support needs, but due to the systemic and attitudinal barriers they experienced (Jindal-Snape et al., 2019).

It is important to also consider the impact of low socioeconomic background on children's primary-secondary school transitions experiences. We found that the household's income, parental education level and area deprivation were all strongly associated with children's experience of transitions. In other words, we found that more children (44%) whose families were in the top income band reported positive transitions as compared to those children (26%) whose families were in the bottom income band (Jindal-Snape et al., 2023). Similarly, parents' education and qualifications also had an impact on their child's transitions experiences. This is of concern also because parents who did not have higher qualifications reported that they had negative experiences in school themselves and were therefore hesitant about going into their child's school (Jindal-Snape & Foggie, 2008). This could suggest a vicious cycle of parents experiencing negative transitions to secondary school which might have an impact on their other educational, professional and life transitions, followed by their children having similar experiences and so on. However, the situation is not as grim as this might suggest. With careful planning, preparation and support all children can be supported to have positive transitions. What is important is that parents who might find it difficult to engage with their child's school or teachers, are supported by other parents and teachers to be able to meaningfully participate and support their child's transitions at home and in school. It is worth considering whether setting up a 'family buddy' system would be better than the 'peer buddy' system that some schools operate, especially in the UK. The peer buddy system is where usually either the current second year or final year students are paired with the new first year students. They meet them weekly and can go to them if looking for support as they are considered to be more accessible and approachable, and can relate to the new student's experiences.

However, what support is available for parents? You might remember when your child started primary school. Parents have opportunities to speak with other parents at the school gates when dropping off or picking up their child. (Or even at birthday parties as parents usually stay when their children are young) A lot of questions that parents might have and are not sure about asking the teacher, can be answered by other parents, whether of children in the same class or other classes. Of course, not all parents are able to be there at either time. If the schools, started a formal system of family buddies as they do with peer buddy, it could mean that the entire family will be connected with another family. Also, if the schools don't, it could be an initiative taken forward by parents themselves, especially as part of the Parent Teacher Association or Parent Council. This might be even more important for families with children with additional support needs where they might feel more comfortable discussing rights and responsibilities with other families who can discuss their first-hand experiences (see Vignette 6.2). Also, if we are mindful of not only the child but also the families' concurrent transitions, families will also be able to receive support for their own transitions.

VIGNETTE 6.2. UNRECOGNISED LABOUR OF PARENTS: MEGAN'S EXPERIENCE

Megan, parent of two autistic children, found that primary-secondary school transitions were even more complex for her children and her.

> Primary-secondary school transitions are hugely complex for all children and parents; the ASN aspect adds extra complexity on top. You can see this from my experience of one autistic child moving to mainstream education (and having a difficult time that is ongoing three years later). I am in the midst of getting my referrals, assessments and reports in a row for requesting a placement in an ASN specialist support base in secondary school, after he has been in mainstream primary education.
>
> If you don't have someone who can tell you the exact phrases, in this new education language, and whom to request what from, you get absolutely nowhere. No matter your rights, the legislation or the responsibilities of the local authority, sadly, the peer support is absolute key to knowing how to move forward.

They also highlighted the isolation as a parent and the importance of peer support for parents.

> But one of the huge factors in our transitions as a parent of autistic children is how over the years you become more and more isolated. As your child progresses through

primary school, the invitations to things such as birthday parties and engagement with out-of-school clubs fall away, because the development of your child is not at the same pace as their peers. This means that any friendships originally forged in early years as parents, also fall away naturally, and unless you know someone through a group or by chance who also has a disabled child, there is nobody who really has much of an idea of the pressures you are under.

Of course, there are specialist support/carers' groups but they aren't focused on educational contexts. A family buddy system might be helpful beyond discussing rights and responsibilities, but in knowing whom to contact and what language to use to access certain types of support.

Megan also highlighted the time, energy and emotion they spent which goes unrecognised.

Around the age of primary-secondary school transitions, there is an enormous moment where lots of people finally truly realise their child isn't going to 'grow out of it', and it is a period of grief and permanent adaptation.

My children's primary-secondary school transitions and ASN have resulted in unrecognised labour, such as the need to learn the language of local authorities and education; the hours put into finding out about laws, rights and responsibilities and coming to understand them in your own context; finding out which third sector or statutory organisations might be able to help; looking for new peer support; seeking referrals and assessments from multiple agencies and keeping a record of all reports. Despite the law, nobody shares this information across agencies. We have to source appropriate educational settings with limited information and no real power. Then the time required for attending meetings, reading minutes, child plans, notes, reports and editing them, advocating and pushing for a larger share of limited resources for your child etc etc. Never mind actually looking after the child in question and remembering to collect them from school!

All of this means that we are forced to forfeit parts of our personal and professional identities – triggering multiple and multi-dimensional transitions for us.

WHY DO I NEED TO BE FAMILIAR WITH RELEVANT LEGISLATION?

Consider Tom's case (Vignette 6.1). Do you believe he has been discriminated against due to his additional support needs? Whose responsibility was it to make sure that the secondary school he was at, was fully accessible? Whose responsibility was it to make sure he was given a range of options when leaving secondary school? Who should take the responsibility for the psychological harm that he experienced?

Most countries have legislations that can, or at least should, support children experiencing additional support needs. For instance, in Scotland, the Education (Additional Support for Learning) (Scotland) Act 2004 (ASL), amended 2009, places specific legislative duties on local authorities in Scotland with clear time scales for transitions planning and practice. They have to request and take account of information and advice from children, families and relevant agencies, at least 12 months prior to starting secondary school. Further, they have to give information to relevant agencies no later than six months prior to the child starting secondary school. This information sharing is crucial to plan transitions so that a child experiencing additional support needs can have successful transitions.

Of course, we can see good examples of the legislation being followed as in Vignette 6.3, with Angie's voice becoming central to decision making. It highlights the importance of us as parents and professionals being aware of the legislation, rights of the child, and the responsibilities that are assigned to us in our roles. However, how easy is the language of the legislation and its implications for the parents, alongside constantly having to advocate for their child and reminding the professionals of their roles and responsibilities? If we consider Megan's experience (see Vignette 6.2), we will be able to understand the complexities that a parent can experience as well as feeling they have no voice.

Similar to Megan, we don't know how many hours of unrecognised labour Angie's parent had to put into Angie having a voice as well, with only the teacher and classmates input being visible to the people in that meeting.

ENHANCED TRANSITIONS

Have you heard of enhanced transitions? Enhanced transitions means that the child might get extra visits to the new school to help with their familiarisation with the school spaces and staff. Also, this provides opportunities for parents also to have meetings with the professionals who will be working with their child to ensure that support is in place for the child in advance of starting the school (e.g., a follow up from Angie's meeting). Figure 6.1 provides an example of that. It should be noted that the child has the **right** to additional visits and **over a period of time**.

Figure 6.1 Enhanced transitions (Source: Jindal-Snape et al., 2022; Art: Monica Burns).

CHILD'S VOICE

You must have heard the term 'voice' or 'child's voice' mentioned multiple times. But what exactly does it mean? There are many ways of explaining it, but we will go with Laura Lundy's (2007) framework as it is very comprehensive. According to her framework, children should have (i) safe and inclusive opportunities to have a voice (space), (ii) we must create ways to facilitate their participation (voice), (iii) we must listen to their voice (audience), and (iv) act based on it (influence). It is important to note that if any of the aspects are missing, then our efforts are meaningless. For instance, if we were to ask you what would you like for dinner, pizza or a chicken pie, and you chose chicken pie, for us to then turn around and say, you know what, that will take a long time to make, let's go with pizza tonight. What would your reaction be? You are likely to say, why did you bother asking me then? If we had made you pizza without asking what you would like to eat, it might be slightly problematic as you weren't given an opportunity for a choice, but it would be more disempowering and frustrating to give that opportunity but not follow through with it. Consider this in the context of child's voice within a school context (and of course it is very important in the home and community context too), what opportunities might they have for having a voice. If we go back to legislation, like the one mentioned earlier, that voice is embedded by law in their transitions to and through secondary school, and post-secondary school. We saw from Tom's experience, neither his, or as far as we can tell, nor his family's, voice was sought or heard (Vignette 6.1). Decisions seemed to have been taken without consultation with them. However, is this always the case? Let's consider Angie's experience (Vignette 6.3).

VIGNETTE 6.3. REVIEW MEETING: NICK'S FIELD NOTES

After prior approval from everyone, I was allowed as a researcher to observe a review meeting between Angie, her family and professionals about her move to the secondary school five months later. The meeting was in a board room in Angie's primary school, with several professionals from different backgrounds and sectors sitting around a very large table. Angie's parents were in the room too. I sat a bit on the side as the observer.

Angie came to the meeting with her guidance teacher and one of her classmates. The people around the table introduced themselves to Angie and her family with names, roles, names of organisations flying around the room. Yikes! I was worried how will Angie and her parents manage to get their voice heard when I was finding so many people in the room a bit overwhelming.

I couldn't be more wrong! Together Angie and her classmate had created a PowerPoint presentation which showed through photos and videos what Angie enjoyed doing, what she was excited about in terms of starting secondary school, what was she concerned about, her dreams, her nightmares… She used her tablet to ask some questions she had about how she would be supported with her educational, social, health transitions etc… these were questions and scenarios that Angie and her parents had been discussing at home for some months too.

Apparently, Angie and her classmate had been working on this presentation for some months with support from their ASN teacher. There was genuine engagement from the professionals. My initial reservations in terms of the formal layout and bigwig professionals were unfounded. With good planning and preparation, it is possible for children to have their voice heard – for others to really listen to them. Holding the meeting in the primary school, a place very familiar to Angie, must have helped too. The mutual partnership and good relationships between Angie, her parents, her classmate and the teacher were front and centre!

The legislation, therefore, provides a clear framework for putting the child at the centre to ensure professionals listen to the child and their family's voice during this process (Jindal-Snape, 2016).

However, it has been reported that some professionals ignore the views of children with additional support needs as they consider it difficult or even impossible to 'get their views' (Dickins, 2008). Here it is important to note that, although it might be framed as the child's inability to have a voice, it is actually the inability of the families or professionals to listen to that voice. So let's think carefully about our roles and responsibilities with regard to children's voice being heard and acted upon. What is your role as a parent? Or if you are a professional coordinating support, what is your role? What is the role of any professional?

In our research, we found that regular and ongoing parent-school communication and engagement were strongly associated with positive transitions experiences (Jindal-Snape et al., 2023). Similarly, Davis et al. (2015) reported that schools that had good partnerships with parents, found that their children had better transitions experiences and it also facilitated the inclusion of their child with additional support needs.

Therefore, it is important for parents and schools to work closely, and more importantly, for the child to have a voice in the transition planning process. This is important so that transitions processes are tailored to meet the diverse needs of each child. There are several creative and playful resources that parents and professionals can use to help listen to their child's voice; a couple have been discussed in this chapter, for others see Chapter 5. However, we should also be mindful that primary-secondary school transitions can trigger additional support need/s for a child, e.g., due to an impact on their emotional wellbeing. Therefore, an ongoing awareness of their emergence and understanding of the need to take action is important. This emerged clearly in Jenny and Lisa's case (Vignette 1.2), and the need for a strong partnership between children, families and professionals became evident.

CHILD-CENTRED PLANNING

Another term you might have heard being mentioned at meetings with professionals is child-centred planning. In simple terms, child-centred planning means that the child and their unique abilities and support needs are the focus of any decisions that will affect them and their life. It also means that professionals will work in partnership with your child and you. This is relevant also in the context of primary-secondary school transitions, with child-centred planning also being embedded in legislation in the UK and elsewhere.

Research suggests that child-centred planning, for every child, is effective as it provides choice and agency to children and meaningful involvement of families. Others have argued that its effectiveness is not fully documented, especially for children living with additional support needs. However, the latter is considered to be due to the planning process not being undertaken as it is meant to be, with limited voice and agency afforded to children and their family. It is important that child-centred planning is an ongoing process with scope for changes made throughout the child's time in school and beyond.

Several approaches and tools have been used to facilitate child or person-centered planning in a range of contexts (Coyle & Lunt, 2010). It is important to note that these are used across age groups and stages of transitions rather than just primary-secondary school transitions. We will discuss two of these approaches here as they are relevant to support primary-secondary school transitions.

i.   Essential Lifestyle Plans (ELP): These have been used to find out what that child needs within the context of their overall life style and is more often used in health contexts. However, these are equally relevant in an educational context.

You can see an example of an ELP in Figure 1 of Martin and Carey's (2009) article. The main headings in their ELP are related to a health related ELP:

a. What/Who is important to X (people, appearance, activities)
b. What is important for X (there is a slight overlap but also includes other aspects such as communication, preference for diet, waking up etc.)
c. People who know X would say… (includes personal attributes such as, loves his family, brilliant swimmer)
d. To keep X stay healthy we must… (a list of strategies are listed)
e. X's nightmares (what X doesn't like or is worried about)
f. To be successful in supporting X we must… (what family and professionals can do)

We have translated these into an ELP for a child to support their primary-secondary school transitions (Figure 6.2). In the main, the important change might be from health in point d. above to 'motivated to learn' or 'for their emotional wellbeing'. Of course, these alternatives might be additional to the six points above rather than replacing d. The crucial point to make here is that the child's voice about all of these aspects is heard and used to develop an ELP, and it

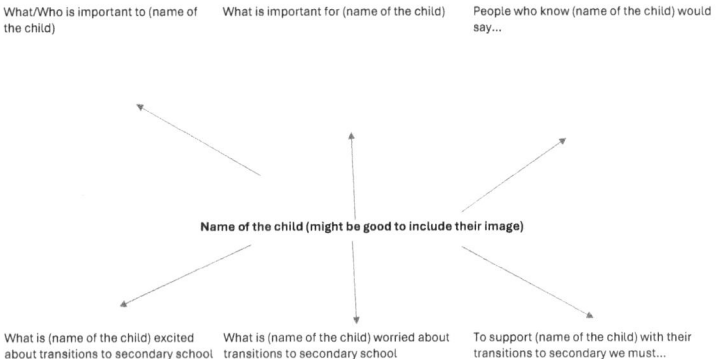

What/Who is important to (name of the child)   What is important for (name of the child)   People who know (name of the child) would say...

Name of the child (might be good to include their image)

What is (name of the child) excited about transitions to secondary school   What is (name of the child) worried about transitions to secondary school   To support (name of the child) with their transitions to secondary we must...

Figure 6.2 ELP template (based on Martin & Carey, 2009).

is then shared with the professionals working with them in primary and secondary schools.You can use this as a template that can be used by parents and/or teachers to work with the child. It is important that it is updated in an ongoing manner as the child's preferences might change in line with developmental and other changes.

(ii) Planning Alternative Tomorrows with Hope (PATH): PATH is a participatory approach that can been used to plan for the next few months or years and ensuring that support systems are available. In this context, PATH might be used with your child to focus on their aspirations for transitions to secondary school and beyond.

The most important aspect of PATH is that it is strengths-based and the child can bring different people from their community (e.g., family, peers, teachers) to support with planning for their aspirations. The community also becomes their support system in planning on how to achieve their aspirations based on where the child is now and what they need to do to actualise their dream. PATH uses graphic illustrations and is colourful. Figure 6.3 provides a template for developing one. Normally you would use a large sheet of paper (or multiple sheets), attach them to a wall and start working on the template. PATH often involves several of the child's significant others and the first step is the child's dream of what they want to achieve, followed by their goal, and then moving to where they are now, who can support them get to their goal and dream, how to stay strong and motivated, with what needs to happen immediately and over a few months. You can view a video about it here Person Centred Planning- PATH meetings (youtube.com)

When facilitated well, child-centred planning approaches ensure that the child's (and families') voice is heard and acted upon.

Figure 6.3 Template to develop PATH.

Organisations working with children have created different resources to support the child and parents with transition planning. You can access some examples here:

https://learningspaces.dundee.ac.uk/esw-transitions-community-library/2023/09/13/compass-online-tool-for-young-people-parents-and-carers-and-professionals/

WILL THE TEACHER THINK A PARENT IS BEING PUSHY IF THEY SUGGEST THEIR INVOLVEMENT IN THEIR CHILD'S TRANSITION PLANS?

Most teachers that we have spoken with over the last 20 years, lament that parents don't get involved in the life of the school or don't respond to their letters or other messages (Jindal-Snape & Foggie, 2008). Therefore, contrary to what you might think, primary and secondary school teachers are keen to interact with the parents, knowing that you are the child's most important support network who can complement any transitions support they are providing in the school, at home. You are the one who understands your child best, and as highlighted in Chapters 2 and 3 what changes are taking place in their behaviour and what that might mean, especially in the context of transitions, emotional wellbeing and mental health.

Across the UK, all schools have either Parent Teacher Associations or Parent Councils with a view to enhance parental involvement. However, at times parental involvement can become a one-way process with *schools deciding* when and how to involve parents and parents hesitating in being pro-active in offering their involvement as they are worried about being considered too pushy. Therefore, more effort is required from you as parents and the teachers to develop a home-school partnership based on a reciprocal relationship of trust, openness and honesty (Jindal-Snape et al., 2012). The board game shared in Chapter 5 can not only facilitate parent-child dialogue but also parent-teacher dialogue. The teacher or parent can use the scenarios in the boxes as cues for discussion about school. The scenarios can be used by parents to make a note of the questions to ask the child's primary/secondary school teacher/s, for example, at parent evenings. Further, this board game can provide an important means of enhancing the child's resilience due to timely and meaningful support being provided in the dialogues generated between the parent-child and parent-teachers.

Like any communication, it is important to be mindful of our tone, frequency and understanding things from the teachers' perspective. Like your child and you, they are also experiencing transitions (see Chapter 7). Using a solution-focussed approach, i.e., instead of going in to discuss problems, also consider what the solution might be, would be useful, especially if you also communicate that you would be happy to be part of providing that solution through partnership working. For instance, when going to the school to talk about your child not being happy at school and what can be done about it, it would be useful to reflect on any recent changes in their behaviour or attitude that might indicate any emotional wellbeing related issues. This is likely to be helpful for the teacher/guidance teacher who might normally only see your child for an hour in a group per week, and that too in a classroom context only.

TOP TIPS FOR CHILDREN FROM CHILDREN

1. Don't worry about going to the new school as you can go there several times before you start studying there.
2. You might want to ask to go at times when other children are not there, so it is a bit quieter.

3. The secondary school might have better facilities, such as specialist software or hardware that you might find useful for learning and communicating.

4. You might find the clear rules and structured timetables of secondary school more useful than the loose structure at your primary school.

5. Practise at home with your family or friends, the questions you would like to ask teachers and guidance team when you are visiting the school.

6. Don't rely on others knowing what you would like or need. It is important for you or your family to be clear with the school about it.

7. It is your right to have positive primary-secondary school transitions!

TOP TIPS FOR PARENTS FROM PARENTS

1. Find a peer group or local organisation that can help you learn about what is available in your area in terms of types of schools, what the law and policies mean in your context, responsibilities of the professionals, as well as the rights your child and you have to ensure positive transitions to secondary school.

2. Ensure that decisions about which secondary school your child will go to are made as early as possible. This includes any placement requests you might want to make for schools that are not automatic routes for children from your child's school.

3. Once you know which school your child will go to, ask the school to organise multiple visits before they move there.

4. Ask both primary and secondary schools to create opportunities for meeting with other parents who are going through these transitions at the same time as you or whose children have already started secondary school.

5. Try out different resources and planning approaches with your child at home, with an emphasis on them being used at school too if they work for your child.

6. Do remember that your child might have emerging additional support needs due to their transitions to, and through, secondary school.

REFERENCES

Coyle, D., & Lunt, J. (2010). Person-centred planning. In P. Talbot, G. Astbury, & T. Mason} (Eds.), *Key Concepts in Learning.* Disabilities (pp. 193–198). SAGE Publications Ltd,.

Davis, J. M., Ravenscroft, J. & Bizas, N. (2015). Transition, inclusion and partnership: Child-, parent- and professional-led approaches in a European research project. *Child Care in Practice*, 21(1), 33–49. https://doi.org/ 10.1080/13575279.2014.976543

Dickins, M. (2008). Listening to young disabled children, Listening as a way of life. national children's bureau. Retrieved from: https://www.ncb.org.uk/ media/74024/listening_to_young_disabled_children.pdf

Dillon, G. V., & Underwood, J. D. M. (2012). Parental perspectives of students with autism spectrum disorders transitioning from primary to secondary school in the United Kingdom. *Focus on Autism and Other Developmental Disabilities*, 27(2), 111–121. https://doi.org/10.1177/ 1088357612441827

Hannah, E. F., & Topping, K. J. (2012). Anxiety levels in students with autism spectrum disorder making the transition from primary to secondary school. *Education and Training in Autism and Developmental Disabilities*, 47(2), 198–209.J-S 2010

Jindal-Snape, D. (2016). *The A–Z of Transitions*. Palgrave Macmillan. https://doi. org/10.1057/978-1-137-52827-8

Jindal-Snape, D., & Cantali, D. (2019). A four-stage longitudinal study exploring pupils' experiences, preparation and support systems during primary–secondary school transitions. *British Educational Research Journal*, 45(6), 1255–1278. https://doi.org/10.1002/berj.3561

Jindal-Snape, D., Bradshaw, P., Gilbert, A., Smith, N., & Knudsen, L. (2023). Primary–secondary school transition experiences and factors associated with differences in these experiences: Analysis of the longitudinal Growing Up in Scotland dataset. *Review of Education*, 11(3), Article e3444. https://doi.org/10.1002/rev3.344

Jindal-Snape, D., & Foggie, J. (2008). A holistic approach to primary - Secondary transitions. *Improving Schools*, 11(1), 5–18. https://doi.org/10.1177/1365480207086750

Jindal-Snape, D., Johnston, B., Pringle, J., Kelly, T., Scott, R., Gold, L., & Dempsey, R. (2019). Multiple and Multidimensional life transitions in the context of life-limiting health conditions: Longitudinal study focussing on perspectives of Young Adults, Families and Professionals. *BMC Palliative Care*, 18, 1–12. Article 30. https://doi.org/10.1186/s12904-019-0414-9

Jindal-Snape, D., Roberts, G., & Venditozzi, D. (2012). Parental involvement, participation and home-school partnership: Using the Scottish lens to explore parental participation in the context of trandsitions. In M. Soininen, & T. Merisuo-Storm (Eds.), *Home-School Partnership in a Multicultural Society* (pp. 73–101). Publications of Turku University Faculty of Education B80.

Lightfoot, L., & Bond, C. (2013). An exploration of primary to secondary school transition planning for children with Down's syndrome. *Educational Psychology in Practice*, 29(2), 163–179. https:// doi.org/10.1080/02667363.2013.800024

Lundy, L. (2007). 'Voice' is not enough: Conceptualising Article 12 of the United Nations convention on the rights of the child. *British Educational Research Journal,* 33(6), 927–942.

Martin, A., & Carey, E. (2009). Person-centred plans: Empowering or controlling?: Person-centred planning with people who have learning disabilities raises issues of power and control. *Learning Disability Practice*, 12(1), 32–37. https://doi.org/10.7748/ldp2009.02.12.1.32.c6856

Neal, S., & Frederickson, N. (2016). ASD transition to mainstream secondary: A positive experience? *Educational Psychology in Practice*, 32(4), 355–373. https://doi.org/10.1080/02667363.2016.1193478

Peters, R., & Brooks, R. (2016). Parental perspectives on the transition to secondary school for students with asperger syndrome and high functioning autism: A pilot survey study. *British Journal of Special Education*, 43(1), 75–91. https://doi.org/10.1111/1467-8578.12125

7

WHAT DO I NEED TO KNOW ABOUT MY OWN TRANSITIONS, AND WHAT SUPPORT COULD BE USEFUL FOR ME?

INTRODUCTION

In this chapter, the last one of this book, we would like to focus on your multiple and multi-dimensional transitions. This is an often forgotten aspect, so we will discuss what parents, carers and teachers need to understand about their transitions. We will follow this with what parents and carers can do to prepare for their child's and/or their own transitions. Finally, we will finish off with top tips for parents and teachers.

DOI: 10.4324/9781032716145-7

WHAT DO SIGNIFICANT OTHERS (PARENTS, CARERS, TEACHERS) NEED TO UNDERSTAND ABOUT THEIR OWN TRANSITIONS?

VIGNETTE 7.1. IMPACT OF SAMMY'S PRIMARY-SECONDARY SCHOOL TRANSITIONS ON THEIR MUM JADE

Jade spoke about her excitement and worries about the changes she herself was going to experience in her relationships with primary school and secondary school. She mentioned a sense of loss at leaving the primary school space, and her concerns were related to the development of new relationships and accessibility of professionals:

If I was worried about anything or wanted the primary school teacher to know that something had happened and to keep an eye on Sammy, I just had to pick up the phone. The office ladies would make sure the teacher got my message or called me back.

Will I be able to do that in the secondary school? There will be so many teachers and even though Sammy will have a guidance teacher, I am not sure I would feel confident talking with them. You hardly get to see them for five minutes at parents' evening! In primary school you developed a good relationship with the teachers and head-teacher. That won't be the same in the bigger school. Also, the size of that school is daunting even for me!

PARENTS AND CARERS' MULTIPLE AND MULTI-DIMENSIONAL TRANSITIONS

Although parents have been identified as one of the most important support systems by children during primary-secondary school transitions, there is hardly any discussion about the transitions these parents will experience as a result of their child starting secondary school. As can be seen in Jade's case, she is navigating her own emotions and potential relationship transitions with the school (Vignette 7.1). On top of that, Sammy is starting secondary school at the same time as some important developmental transitions (Eccles et al., 1993). The developmental transitions, i.e., puberty, come along with children exerting independence, including that from their parents (see Chapter 1 for more details). This is likely to involve a change in the dynamics between Sammy and Jade, leading to the need for Jade to adapt to this change in her relationship with Sammy. For instance, although Sammy was grateful that Jade had driven them to the secondary school for the first few weeks, they categorically refused a lift from her after that and wanted to make their own way to school even though it meant taking two buses and leaving home early. This required Jade to re-negotiate her dynamics with Sammy as well as to re-negotiate her start time at work with her boss who had agreed to her starting her shift at 9:30 am to give her time to drop Sammy off. The latter then had an impact on the work schedule of her colleagues.

Therefore, children's diverse types of transitions will trigger transitions of their parents, and that of those connected to them. Similarly, as parents you will be experiencing your own unrelated transitions. For instance a parent might be experiencing some transitions in their workplace due to staff being made redundant or their parents requiring additional support due to their emerging health needs. These then will have an impact on their availability for their child, whether physical or emotional, and trigger transitions for them. Similarly, if your child's emotional wellbeing is affected due to any of their transitions, it might also affect your emotional wellbeing even before we consider the impact of your unrelated transitions.

This interaction of child's and parents' transitions, and ongoing, multiple and complex transitions has been explained using the metaphor of a Rubik's cube. This metaphor has been used to explain a research-based theory, Multiple and Multi-dimensional Transitions (MMT) Theory (Jindal-Snape, 2016, 2018, 2023). Let's imagine that the yellow colour represents Alex and his significant others, such as mother, father, Maths teacher, friends and guidance teacher. And that red represents Sammy and their significant others, blue represents Jenny and so on. Any change in the yellow face of the Rubik's cube will lead to changes for the remaining yellow too. Similarly, when we move any colour or line of the Rubik's cube, it doesn't just change that line on one face of the Rubik's cube; it changes it for the remaining five too. This then leads to the situation of one person's transitions triggering transitions for everyone in that child's ecological system. You must be wondering what is an ecological system? Briefly, Bronfenbrenner (1979) developed the Ecological Systems Theory to explain that different systems, whether close to an individual (e.g., family) or at a distance (e.g., educational policy), are likely to be interconnected and have an impact on that individual.

However, the situation is even more complex as we haven't taken into account ecological systems of significant others in each child's ecological system as they might not be the same as that of the child. For instance, as mentioned earlier, Jade's ecological system includes Sammy, her parents, boss and work colleagues. Sammy's transitions are triggering transitions for significant others in Jade's ecological system. Similarly, these people in their ecological system will be experiencing their own transitions. Their transitions will then trigger the child's transitions too.

Along with this, the child or family or professionals are situated in an ever-changing dynamic environment. This became really obvious during COVID (see Figure 7.1) which had an impact on all types of transitions or what some have referred to as 'disrupted transitions'. We don't agree with the terminology of 'disrupted transitions'; it is important to note that transitions will happen not only due to *change* but also can happen due to the *change they had expected not happening*.

Figure 7.1 Multiple and multi-dimensional transitions of a professional and family (Copyright: Divya Jindal-Snape, Art: Clio Ding, Source: Jindal-Snape et al., 2022).

Figure 7.1 shows a nurse, Kate, who was working in a COVID ward standing on one side of the cube (please note only Kate's eco-system is shown and we have used multiple colours on the cube for illustration purposes only). She was working long hours and returned home around her daughter's bedtime. Further, once she came back home, she had a shower before interacting with her family. Her professional transitions were having a direct impact on her personal transitions as a mother and wife as she was not able to spend the time she normally did with her family. Her professional transitions triggered transitions for the rest of the family too. Her daughter was having psychological transitions as she was too young to understand why 'mummy' wasn't there to have dinner with them or read her bedtime stories. Her husband worked from home to support their daughter and also carried on undertaking his job and all the housework. He also went to drop the weekly shop at his in-laws' doorstep as they were shielding. These multiple roles meant that he had to juggle a lot of different things which required adaptations and led to multiple transitions, across the contexts of home, workplace, community. Kate's parents were experiencing their own transitions, some due to Kate but some unrelated such as having to shield during COVID limiting their normal activities which led to emotional and social transitions for them, along with an impact on their emotional wellbeing.

Therefore, applying this to our own context, it is clear that the child and significant others are likely to experience multiple transitions at the same time. The multi-dimensional transitions highlight the interaction of the child's different transitions, i.e., the child might have made good friends and have successful relationship transitions but might be finding academic transitions to be less successful. These interactions might support the child with the successful transitions providing a buffer for the less successful ones with a positive impact on their emotional wellbeing (see Educational and Life Transitions model, Jindal-Snape & Ingram, 2013).

Further, the multi-dimensional transitions also refer to the interaction of the child's and significant others' transitions. This highlights the importance of *parents, carers and teachers* not only understanding the child's multiple and multi-dimensional transitions, but also *their own* multiple and multi-dimensional transitions. Consider the guidance we are provided during safety briefings before a plane takes off. We are asked to put on our oxygen masks first in the case of an emergency before assisting anyone else. And although we are listening to the advice from the flight attendant and thinking there is no way I won't put the oxygen mask on my child first, we know that there is a reason that their advice makes sense and will lead to better chances of the child and us surviving. This applies quite appropriately to our transitions context; if we are having difficulties managing our own multiple transitions, we might find it difficult to support the child with their transitions. At the very least, an awareness and understanding of our own transitions and transitions support needs are important, as is the potential impact of it on our and their emotional wellbeing.

TEACHERS' MULTIPLE AND MULTI-DIMENSIONAL TRANSITIONS

It is also important to consider teachers' transitions. Similar to you, your child's transitions will trigger transitions for the teachers too. Further, you will be facilitating one child's transitions, they will be managing those of 30 plus children in just one year group. Remember transitions are ongoing so all children in every year group will be experiencing a range of transitions with each teacher providing different types of support to them. Further, as we saw in Kate's case (Figure 7.1), alongside professional transitions, they will have unrelated personal transitions, triggering amongst others, psychological, relationship, social and identity transitions. Unfortunately, teachers can be so focused on your child's transitions that they don't consider their own transitions and have reported that children's primary-secondary school transitions didn't trigger transitions for them. This is despite acknowledging that letting go of previous pupils (and sets of parents) feels like a loss, and that they are excited about working with new pupils. The latter is despite a lot of work and time being spent on adapting their practices to meet the needs of the new pupils (and sets of parents) (Jindal-Snape & Cantali, 2019).

Further, we are also aware from our research that teachers are not provided adequate training at the university or during subsequent professional development on facilitating primary-secondary school transitions. This is worrying as they are being asked to take another role but left to their own devices to provide the best practices and support.

Despite this, teachers are looking to innovate within the constraints of time and resources, leading to educational and professional transitions for them. Several interesting examples of this were seen during COVID-19 and teachers have mentioned in our research that it was an eye opener for them. Instead of repeating the same induction and familiarisation activities they did year after year, because that was what had always happened, they had to stop and think the purpose of transitions planning and preparation, and how best to provide support to children and families (Edge et al., 2023). These, according to them, resulted in better and more accessible online and multi-media practices, that children and parents could access whenever they wanted to rather than it being determined by the school as a linear transitions process. They were able to create virtual tours narrated by children whose perspectives were likely to be closer to those of the children starting secondary school. These two quotes emphasise how this became a game changer for them.

> …face to face meetings, they've moved online now and actually been far more successful as a result, because we had more of them… the flexibility… you're not limited to an hour when you're in school, you've got your half an hour here, half an hour there when you can focus on specific things. (Transition Lead, School J, Wales, FSM 31−40%)
>
> (Edge et al., 2023, p. 23)

> … we filmed around about a 40 minute video and it's on (our) YouTube channel… each department filmed a little section, so we went viral on that with … science had done it like brainiac, history had done it like Horrible Histories, so every year we try and go viral. (Transition Lead, School D, England, FSM 41−50%)
>
> (Edge et al., 2023, p. 23)

Understanding each other's multiple and multi-dimensional transitions can help us see each other as equal partners in supporting the child's multiple and multi-dimensional transitions. A bit of self-compassion and compassion towards each other on parents' and teachers' part is required (Jindal-Snape, 2023; Pillar 2: Multiple and Multi-Dimensional Transitions Habits of Heart).

HOW CAN PARENTS BETTER PREPARE THEMSELVES FOR THEIR CHILD'S AND THEIR OWN TRANSITIONS?

In other chapters, we have focussed on how the significant others, especially the parents, can prepare their child for their primary-secondary school transitions. Here we will focus on how you can prepare yourself for your child's and your own transitions. The most important transitions you are likely to experience during your child's primary-secondary school transitions are identity transitions (changing roles/expectations) and relationship transitions (e.g., with your child, family members, primary/secondary school, other parents). For instance, Jade had to prepare herself for managing Sammy's educational and developmental transitions.

Let us use the metaphor of tango to understand the relationship between our child and us. One takes a step forward, the other takes a step back, you swap and so on. If both decide to move forward at the same time without considering the other person's moves, you are likely to step on each other's toes. These successful and unsuccessful tango moves have probably happened to all of us as parents, carers and teachers. Or we can remember them from when we were 11–12 years old in our interaction with parents and others. How this relationship develops over this crucial period in their life means we have to look out for cues from them, about their emotional wellbeing, mental health, behaviours. As a parent, as we found in our research, at times it easy to 'let go' of our identity when we were the parent that the child used to depend on for their every single need (Jindal-Snape et al., 2019). However, if we understand that due to our child's transitions, we will have identity transitions, relationship transitions and psychological transitions, maybe it is easier to prepare for them, and without any negative impact on our own emotional wellbeing.

Further, you are likely to experience psychological transitions due to your identity and relationship transitions. It is important for you to acknowledge your own feelings and emotions about your child's and your own transitions. Elsewhere we talked about the importance of open communication with your child to support their emotional wellbeing and transitions (Chapter 3). This applies to you too. Please openly communicate your own emotions in discussions with them (without overwhelming them or passing on your concerns about their transitions) and other family members or even other parents you know as they are likely to be experiencing similar transitions. (*Although please be mindful that everyone's transitions experiences will be different due to the interaction of their multiple and multi-dimensional transitions, and context.*) Remember the scenario we discussed earlier of putting your own oxygen mask first? If your own psychological transitions and emotional wellbeing are affected, you will not be able to support your child with theirs.

Also, transitions mean adapting to change/s over time; therefore, don't expect to get everything right the first time! This might be the time when you have to learn to be more self-compassionate (Jindal-Snape, 2023; 'Pillar 2:' Multiple and Multi-Dimensional Transitions Habits of Heart) and have a growth mindset, where you move forward knowing that it is ok not to have got it right this time but you can the next time (Jindal-Snape, 2023; 'Pillar 3: Multiple and Multi-dimensional Transitions Attitudes and beliefs about transitions and your ability to navigate them).

Schools can also prepare you for your child's transitions as well as your own by working with you in partnership, by understanding and acknowledging that you are the most important support net-work of children during primary-secondary school transitions (see Chapter 1; Jindal-Snape & Cantali, 2019). The more information parents receive beforehand, the more prepared they can be for their own (changing) role and 'letting go' along with other related and unrelated multiple transitions.

TOP TIPS FOR PARENTS FROM PARENTS

1. Be self-compassionate as managing your own transitions can be hard enough without supporting your child with theirs.
2. Be mindful of your own transitions support needs and access support for them.
3. Ask other parents for support – it is nothing to be ashamed of. You will find other parents will be really pleased that you have started that process so they can get support from you too.
4. Equally, be mindful that everyone will be experiencing multiple transitions, and their support needs might be unmet. Be compassionate when they behave in ways you have not experienced before.
5. Similarly, be mindful of your own changing behaviours, emotions, energy levels, as they might be indicative of a decline in your emotional wellbeing.
6. Be open and honest in communicating your feelings with your child and rest of the family. This might build a trusting and open relationship with your child, along with you being able to process your emotions.
7. Remember that if your first strategy at supporting your or your child's transitions doesn't work, you have plenty of time to strategise and try new ways of supporting them and yourself. This applies to your and their emotional wellbeing too.
8. Be proactive! Contact schools and teachers if you need information or advice. Most would welcome that.

TOP TIPS FOR TEACHERS TO SUPPORT PARENTS' TRANSITIONS

1. Understand and acknowledge that parents are also experiencing multiple transitions as a result of their child's transitions as well as their other transitions.
2. During primary-secondary transitions, it is possible that parents will need support with their emotional wellbeing along with

their child. Consider beforehand the resources or information about sources of support they can access if that is the case.

3. Organise informal and formal visits for parents to the secondary school over time.

4. Organise formal parent networking events.

5. Support parents, parent councils and/or Parent Teacher Associations in organising informal networking events.

6. Adopt a system of parent/family buddies where families are matched with each other rather than just the children.

7. Value their role as parents and involve them as partners in the transitions process.

8. Ensure there is an effective two-way communication with parents. It is not about parents passively receiving information.

9. Seek parental input in the information that is shared between schools about their child. This will provide information about other aspects related to home/community and other transitions their child might be experiencing.

10. Provide parents with opportunities to meet with staff working with their child.

11. Support parents in understanding the legislative obligations of schools and local authorities and children/parents' rights, especially for children with additional support needs.

12. Support parents in understanding their own transitions and provide information that can help facilitate their successful transitions.

TOP TIPS FOR TEACHERS FROM TEACHERS

1. Be aware and self-compassionate as the children's transitions will trigger transitions for you too. Further, this will lead to your own transition support needs so proactively seek clear mechanism of organisational support for this.

2. Undertake regular reciprocal visits to primary/secondary schools to interact with children and other professionals.

3. Consider setting up a teacher buddy system and shadow them across stages. The buddy can become an important support network of yours, especially to support you with your transitions and emotional wellbeing.
4. Ask your schools/local authority education department to create of transitions teams that can provide support to teachers with transitions planning and preparation for children, parents and teachers.
5. Ask your school to invest in your ongoing professional development that can provide you with an understanding of 'best' transitions practices for children, parents and yourself.

REFERENCES

Bronfenbrenner, U. (1979). *The Ecology of Human Development: Experiments by Nature and Design*. Harvard University Press.

Eccles, J. S., Midgley, C. Wigfield, A. Buchanan, C. M., Reuman, D., Flanagan, C., & Mac Iver, D. (1993). Development during adolescence: The impact of stage environment fit in young adolescents' experiences in schools and families. *American Psychologist*, 48, 90–101.

Edge, D., Redwood, S., Jindal-Snape, D., & Crawley, E. (2023). Impact of COVID-19 pandemic on secondary school teaching staff and primary to secondary transitions. *Psychology in the Schools*, 61(1), 17–28. https://doi.org/10.1002/pits.23017

Jindal-Snape, D. (2016). *The A–Z of Transitions*. Palgrave Macmillan. https://doi.org/10.1057/978-1-137-52827-8

Jindal-Snape, D. (2018). Transitions from early years to primary and primary to secondary schools in Scotland. In T. Bryce, W. Humes, D. Gillies, & A. Kennedy (Eds.), *Scottish Education* (5th ed.). Edinburgh University Press.

Jindal-Snape, D. (2023). Multiple and multi-dimensional educational and life transitions: Conceptualization, theorization and XII pillars of transitions. In R. J. Tierney, F. Rizvi, & K. Erkican (Eds.), *International Encyclopedia of Education* (Fourth Edition) (4th ed., pp. 530–543). Elsevier. https://doi.org/10.1016/B978-0-12-818630-5.14060-6

Jindal-Snape, D., & Cantali, D. (2019). A four-stage longitudinal study exploring pupils' experiences, preparation and support systems during primary-secondary school transitions. *British Educational Research Journal*, 45(6), 1255–1278. https://doi.org/10.1002/berj.3561

Jindal-Snape, D., & Ingram, R. (2013). Understanding and supporting triple transitions of international doctoral students: ELT and SuReCom models. *Journal of Perspectives in Applied Academic Practice*, 1(1), 17 24. https://jpaap.napier.ac.uk/index.php/JPAAP/article/view/39

Jindal-Snape, D., Johnston, B., Pringle, J., Kelly, T., Scott, R., Gold, L., & Dempsey, R. (2019). Multiple and Multidimensional life transitions in the context of life-limiting health conditions: Longitudinal study focussing on perspectives of Young Adults, Families and Professionals. BMC *Palliative Care*, 18, 1–12. Article 30. https://doi.org/10.1186/s12904-019-0414-9

Jindal-Snape, D. (Ed.), Murray, C. (Ed.), Innes, N. (Ed.), Tooman, T., Al-Yaseen, W., Herd, D., Ding, C., Corrales, M., & Teo Lewen, J. (2022). *THE COVID ROLLERCOASTER: Multiple and Multi-dimensional Transitions of Healthcare Graduates*. UniVerse. https://doi.org/10.20933/100001247

GLOSSARY

Attentional Control Theory: outlines how our ability to concentrate is impacted by feelings of anxiety, leading to cognitive interference through competing task-irrelevant thoughts (e.g., self-preoccupation, worry).

Cognitive interference: when our attention (including our ability to focus, process information and problem-solve) is interrupted and reduced.

Coping efficacy: an internal resilience resource that refers to an individual's appraisals and sense of control in being able to manage the demands of a stressful situation and emotions aroused to cope.

Diathesis–Stress Model: a psychological framework used to explain how mental health disorders develop as a result of the interaction between an individual's biology, genes and individual make-up (diathesis), in addition to their environment, including family background, society and life experiences.

Emotional wellbeing: a dimension of our wellbeing, which is concerned with hedonia (e.g., positive and negative affect and life satisfaction; 'feeling well') and eudaimonia (e.g., welfare and functioning, 'doing well').

Eudaimonic wellbeing: often referred to as objective wellbeing and is based on assumptions about human needs (e.g., physical health), rights (e.g., adequate education) and life circumstances (e.g., work-life balance), and an individual flourishing and functioning across these domains, e.g., 'doing well'.

Hedonic wellbeing: often referred to as subjective wellbeing, and is concerned with an individual's self-evaluation, both cognitively in terms of their life satisfaction, and affectively, through the prevalence of positive vs. negative emotions, e.g., 'feeling well'.

Intervention: a planned programme or strategy designed to improve a targeted outcome, e.g., in behaviour, performance.

Locus of control: the extent to which people feel that they can control the events that affect them.

Longitudinal: this refers to research carried out over a long period of time, usually with the same participants, to find out whether outcomes change or whether they are consistent.

Multiple and Multi-dimensional Transitions (MMT) Theory: a holistic framework for understanding the transitions experiences of individuals and their significant others.

Resilience: the ability to manage challenge, setback and change to adapt and maintain positive emotional wellbeing by drawing on protective resources within ourselves (e.g., this could be coping skills) and our environments (e.g., supportive relationships).

Scale: a standardised system of measuring something within a questionnaire.

Self-efficacy: an individual's subjective evaluation of their ability to successfully perform specific actions.

Self-esteem: an individual's subjective evaluation of their competence, worth and value.

Stage–Environment Fit Theory: outlines the importance of the *match* between children's developing needs and their social environment.

Strength-model of self-control: outlines how an individual's ability to cope deteriorates as the number of stressors in their life accumulates, co-exists and persists.

Transitions: a complex, ongoing process of adaptations triggered by any changes in domains (e.g., psychological, educational) and contexts (e.g., home, school). Transitions affect not only the individual (both positively and negatively) but also their significant others, such as family, peers, and professionals, and require ongoing support.

Wellbeing: a multidimensional concept, underpinned by multiple schools of thought from psychology, public health and economics (to name a few), reflecting the holistic objective and subjective experience of positive functioning and satisfaction across multiple areas of life.

For Product Safety Concerns and Information please contact our EU
representative GPSR@taylorandfrancis.com
Taylor & Francis Verlag GmbH, Kaufingerstraße 24, 80331 München, Germany